On Common GROUND

Worktext B

Project Manager and Editorial Director: Roseanne Mendoza
Editorial Associates: Jane Belenky Smith and Sally Conover
Photo Researcher: Gina Nonnenmacher
Cover art and design-related art: Jane O'Neal
Photographs from the *On Common Ground* series: Jane O'Neal
Artwork and maps: Max McDonald
Production/Electronic art: PC&F, Inc.
Acquired photos: See Photo Credits, pp. 179 and 180

Manufactured in the United States of America.

ISBN: 1-58370-051-X

03 02 01 00 5 4 3 2

On Common Ground
Worktext B

Writers

Sally Beaty

K. Lynn Savage

Beth Robinson

Kathleen Santopietro Weddel

Content Specialists

Roy Erickson

David Vigilante

IN·TELE·COM
INTELLIGENT TELECOMMUNICATIONS®

Pasadena, California 91105

Table of Contents

Worktext B

Turning Points	Find Out More	Inside Information
Playing fair—what due process of law means	<ul><li>The Constitution and due process</li><li>Individual rights versus the rights of society</li></ul>	The Judicial Branch of Government
Reasons for due process of law	<ul><li>How the Constitution protects the rights of people accused of crimes</li></ul>	The Money System in the United States
Steps in a trial	<ul><li>Steps government must follow to protect the rights of the accused</li></ul>	Facts about Different States within the United States
Expansion of the right to vote	<ul><li>The election process</li></ul>	Qualifications of Elected Officials
Historical concepts that are the basis of the U.S. political system	<ul><li>Democracy in ancient Athens</li><li>Representative government in Rome</li><li>The English tradition</li></ul>	*The Pledge of Allegiance*
Steps for removing elected officials who break their contract of trust with the people	<ul><li>How citizens can use their political power</li><li>People's rights and responsibilities</li><li>Differences between democracies and dictatorships</li></ul>	*The Star-Spangled Banner*
Reasons for immigration; economic contributions of immigrants	<ul><li>Economic powers that the Constitution gives Congress</li><li>Economic rights of the people</li></ul>	Geography and Jobs
How social and political change occurs in the United States	<ul><li>Court rulings on discrimination</li><li>Legislation</li></ul>	Holiday Traditions

Acknowledgments

Developing a product of the magnitude and complexity of *On Common Ground* requires the dedicated, creative, and collaborative efforts of many people, working in tandem over a prolonged period of time. Only a few of their names can be singled out in the few lines that follow, but our gratitude to the team as a whole should be read into every word.

Special appreciation is extended to the

- ▶ leadership of INTELECOM, to members of the Board of Directors and Executive Committee, whose belief in the *On Common Ground* project gave it life
- ▶ United States Department of Justice, Immigration and Naturalization Service, and the Departments of Education of California, Florida, and New York for critical developmental and financial support
- ▶ National Leadership Council for Distance Learning and Adult Education and the U.S. Department of Education for taking the lead in developing the infrastructure to optimize distributed learning options for adults through the use of telecommunications technologies
- ▶ Center for Civic Education and Charles N. Quigley, Executive Director, for contributing the basic ideas of American constitutional democracy set forth in the Center's *We the People, The Citizen and the Constitution*
- ▶ National Center for History in the Schools, the Curriculum Task Force and the National Council for History Standards for guidance in developing the Turning Points segments and the worktexts
- ▶ video production team that did not back away from creating rich episodes that engage and challenge learners

The National Standards for Civics and Government and the National Standards for United States History provided the conceptual framework for *On Common Ground*. The major themes for the series—recommended by state leaders responsible for citizenship education, master teachers, and curriculum specialists— were reviewed by key government leaders, public officials, and immigration policy specialists including Dr. Lawrence Fuchs, Brandeis University, whose insights and suggestions were particularly valuable.

As the series moved into production, *On Common Ground* was shaped and molded, episode-by-episode and chapter-by-chapter, by the National Academic Council. This distinguished panel of educators—specialists in the fields of civics, history, and adult education—includes

- ▶ GLENDA ANDERSON—Adult Education Coordinator, ESOL and ABE, for 16 Technical, Adult and Community Education Centers, Orange County Public Schools Workforce Education Department, Florida
- ▶ ROY ERICKSON—Director of Justice Education Programs for the Center for Civic Education; California Coordinator for the Center's *We the People, the Citizen and the Constitution*; author; program director for major grant projects; past president of the National Social Studies Supervisors Association
- ▶ PATRICIA MOONEY GONZALEZ—ESOL Specialist, New York State Department of Education, Office of Workforce Preparation and Continuing Education; academic advisor and co-author of Worktexts and Photo Stories for *Crossroads Café*
- ▶ BETH ROBINSON—principal consultant, Adult Education and Even Start for her state; leader in developing programs that serve immigrants and refugees

- ADRIANA SANCHEZ-ALDANA—ESL/Citizenship Resource Teacher for Sweetwater Union High School District, California; developer of training package used throughout the state to educate teachers and tutors new to citizenship instruction
- K. LYNN SAVAGE—Instructor, City College of San Francisco; author and curriculum designer; lead academic advisor for *Crossroads Café*, teacher training specialist; 1998 recipient of Heinle & Heinle Publishers' Lifetime Achievement Award
- DAVID VIGILANTE—Associate Director, National Center for History in the Schools; member, Curriculum Task Force that developed History Standards; co-editor of *Bring History Alive!*; developer of curricular materials for National Center, Library of Congress, Huntington Library, and New York Times *Live from the Past* series
- KATHLEEN SANTOPIETRO WEDDEL—Adult Basic Education consultant for the Colorado Department of Education and others; author of skill-based textbooks and teacher training materials

Three members of the Council—Lynn Savage, Beth Robinson, and Kathy Santopietro Weddel— accepted the responsibility of developing the *On Common Ground* worktexts with Sally Beaty. Their creativity and commitment are reflected n the pages of this worktext. So, too, is the help and advice they received from other members of the NAC, as they linked the key concepts of each episode's dramatic story and documentary to the printed word—reinforcing the lesson's themes, fostering inquiry, and extending learning.

The transformation of the manuscript to finished product was guided by Roseanne Mendoza, who played a dual role as editorial director and production manager with extraordinary skill. She was ably assisted in this process by Jane Belenky Smith of INTELECOM and Sally Conover, ESL specialist. The production stills captured by Jane O'Neal, the imaginative sketches of Max McDonald, and the indefatigable photo research of Gina Nonnenmacher added immeasurably to the finished product.

Heartfelt appreciation to each of you, named and unnamed, who made *On Common Ground* a reality!

Sally Beaty, President
INTELECOM

These pages explain what the *On Common Ground* program is and how to use it. If you are not sure about how to use the program after you read this material, ask someone to discuss it. If you start with a clear idea of how to use *On Common Ground*, your chances for success will be excellent.

What Is *On Common Ground*?

On Common Ground is a different and exciting way to learn about U.S. history and government. If you are new to the United States, it is also an excellent way to gain the knowledge necessary to pass the citizenship test. In this learning venture, the television episodes will show you democracy in action. The worktexts will help you understand the key concepts—the most important ideas behind those actions.

The Television Episodes

Each of the 15 thirty-minute episodes includes an action-filled story and a short documentary segment. The stories take place in a typical American city. They show the "common ground"—the common values that people in the United States share. You will see the difference that individuals can make by exercising their rights as citizens. But each story is more than just an interesting drama. It is also an example of a concept that is central to American democracy.

The pictures below show the main characters in the stories.

The Worktexts

There are two worktexts that provide learning activities related to the television episodes. Worktext A includes Episodes 1 through 7; Worktext B includes Episodes 8 through 15. The worktexts help you better understand what you hear and see in the videos. They also provide more information and activities so that you can be an active learner by thinking, talking, reading, and writing about what you hear and see.

How Do I Use the Video Programs?

Watch each episode again and again. If you are watching the programs on television, you can record them and watch as many times as you like. The television programs and videos have closed captions, so that you can see the words the characters say on the screen. Watch without the captions first to get the general idea. Try to guess the meaning of words you don't understand. Then, if you need to see those words, watch again with the captions on.

Questions

Here are some questions learners often ask about *On Common Ground*.

Carla Castillo
TV News Reporter

Marty Siegel
Assistant District
Attorney

Diane Clayton
Community Relations

Derek Powell
Assistant to the Mayor

Jess Holcomb
City Attorney

Jenny Tang
Receptionist

Mayor Reilly

What Do the Liberty Bells Mean?

The Worktext activities are marked with one, two, or three liberty bells that indicate three levels of difficulty.

In each section of the worktext, do as many of the different level activities as you can. For example, in "Remember the Story," maybe you can do the level-one and the level-two activities easily. However, you may not be able to complete the level-three activity. So stop after the second level and move to the next section, "Remember Turning Points." Maybe here you can do all three levels easily, or you may be able to do only the level-one activity. But always begin with the level-one activity. And remember—if you have problems with an activity, get help from your teacher, tutor, study partner, or someone else.

If I Need Help, Where Do I Go?

Work with a study partner—another learner, relative, friend, neighbor, or coworker. Your study partner can be someone who knows more English or more about U.S. history and government than you do. But anyone who is interested in talking about the ideas in *On Common Ground* can be a good study partner. Here are three things you can do with your partner:

▶ Talk about the video story.
▶ Ask questions about things you don't understand.
▶ Compare your activity answers and share your ideas and experiences.

What Do I Need to Know About Using Each Section in the Worktexts?

The worktexts have activities for you to do before and after you watch each episode. Here are some suggestions for using the different sections in the worktexts.

Before You Watch

These sections will introduce what happens in the story and the ideas presented in "Turning Points."

First, study the picture or pictures on the *opening page* of the unit. What do you think the story is about? Next, read the information below the picture.

Look at the six pictures on the "Preview the Story" page. These pictures provide an idea of what the story is about. Then read the questions and think about the answers you would give before you turn on your television set

Read the information and look at the pictures in "Preview Turning Points." Think about the questions

at the bottom of the page and share your answers with your study partner or someone else who is interested in the series.

After You Watch

After "Remember the Story," you will do these activities.

🔔 Read what people said, then write who said it to whom. This helps you remember people in the story and why they are important.

🔔 🔔 Read several paragraphs that tell the story and put them in order. Then match underlined words in the paragraphs with their definitions. These words will help you understand key concepts.

🔔 🔔 🔔 Work with a partner to role-play a conversation between two people from the story.

In the next section of the worktext, "Remember Turning Points," you will do these activities.

🔔 Check whether you understand information from Turning Points by marking sentences true or false, matching items, or categorizing items.

🔔 🔔 Put words and phrases into a chart or timeline that shows how something you heard or read is organized.

🔔 🔔 🔔 Complete a chart using your own words and adding new information from your experience or your learning.

"Making Connections" will help you connect the story to "Turning Points."

Getting Additional Information

"Find Out More" is a section with a reading and activities that expand on the theme of the unit. Work through this section following these steps:

▶ In "Find Out More: Reading," look at the illustrations and read the section headings. Think about the questions and ask yourself what the reading could be about.
▶ Read the selection. After you finish each section, try to answer the question in your own words.
▶ Notice how the words in darker type in the reading are used. Try to guess what each word means. Check your definitions against the glossary in the back of the book. For extra practice, you may want to make a new sentence with each word.
▶ Finally, answer the questions in "Find Out More: Key Ideas."

"Inside Information" focuses on topics such as holidays, qualifications to hold elected office, or U.S. coins with famous people on them. This is an activity to have fun with—often a crossword puzzle, a word search, or a short, interesting reading.

Using the Information

In "Pick Your Project," you choose from three different activities and share your results.

 In *Community Matters: Interact!,* you will get information by talking to someone from a government agency or by watching a process related to government, like a trial. These activities are good for people who learn best by listening and talking.

In *In the News: Get the Facts!,* you will get information from reading newspapers or magazines or from listening to the news on radio or television. These activities are good for people who like to work alone and who learn best by thinking or analyzing.

In *Creative Works: React!,* you will have a chance to add your creativity to the theme of the unit. These activities are good for people who learn well from artistic and visual projects.

Check Your Own Learning

Several sections at the end of the worktext help you check your learning after completing each episode.

After each activity, always use the "Answers for Exercises" to check your answers. When you miss an answer, review the video or worktext.

When you finish a unit, turn to the "Score Sheet for Answers for Exercises" and record your points. If you are part of a class, your teacher may want to see your scores for the exercises to help you with the answers you missed.

After you watch an episode and complete the worktext exercises for it, do the "Check Your Progress" section for that episode. This check-up review has three parts for the different levels.

In *Check Your Memory,* you will answer questions about key government, history, and civics concepts in the episode.

In *Make it Real,* you will use what you learned in the episode to explain an event or situation. To do this, you need to understand the key concepts you hve been exploring.

And in *You Be the Judge,* you will solve a problem by selecting the better of two solutions and then writing one more. These are interesting situations to talk about with a partner after you check your answers in "Answers for Check Your Progress" and record your score.

When you finish "Check Your Progress," turn to the "Answers for Check Your Progress" section for that episode. For any key concept questions you missed in "Check Your Memory," study the information in the *Review* column of the answer key. If you have questions, talk about them with your teacher. Then record your scores on the "Score Sheet for Answers for Check Your Progress."

In the "Rate Yourself" section, read the unit objectives and check how much you learned. Be honest when you answer. Your answers will tell your teacher or study partner if you need more help.

At the end of your worktext, you also will find a copy of the U.S. Constitution and a glossary of important terms. As you read or review those sections, always check the meaning of words related to law and government in this glossary.

8 Rules of the Game

The Constitutional Amendments state that no person shall be deprived of life, liberty, or property without due process of law.

In this episode, a man convicted of an ATM robbery fights to prove his innocence, and two other men are accused of selling drugs.

What rights do these people have?

1

Preview the Story

Look at the pictures from each story. Think about these questions. Share your ideas with someone.

What do you see?

What are these people thinking? What are they feeling?

What do you think will happen?

Anwar Khalil's Story

The Police Officers' Story

Preview Turning Points

The concept of *due process of law* is an important part of the Constitution. Due process means that government cannot interfere with a person's right to life, liberty, or property without good and fair reasons.

Think about the ideas above as you look at the pictures.

Think about these questions. Share your answers with someone.

In these pictures, when is government involved? What is its role?

When should government not be involved in people's lives?

Why is it important for government to act in ways that are fair and reasonable for all people?

Remember the Story

Anwar Khalil's Story

🔔 **Read what people said. Look at the pictures. Complete the chart.**

Katherine Morrison
News Anchor

Marilyn Corbin
Defense Attorney

Jury

Judge

Anwar Khalil
Defendant

TV audience

Barbara Weaver
Defense witness

What People Said	Who Said It	To Whom
1. "This is a terrible mistake. I did not commit this crime."	*Anwar Khalil*	*Judge*
2. "Although he was positively identified in the line-up, Khalil maintained that he was not the person recorded on camera."		
3. "After you hear the evidence, you will have the opportunity to allow an innocent man to reclaim his life."		
4. "I was never interviewed by detectives at all."		
5. "What should outrage this jury is that the police were under so much pressure to make an arrest that they never bothered to locate Miss Weaver."		

🔔 🔔 **Put the paragraphs in order. Number them 1 to 5.**

_____ a. Anwar Khalil testifies that he was at a sports lounge the night of the robbery. Barbara Weaver verifies his story. It was her last night of work at the lounge, and she remembers Khalil because of his accent.

_____ b. The jury reaches its <u>verdict</u>. Anwar Khalil is not guilty of the charges. The jury <u>acquits</u> him. In the end, Anwar Khalil feels that there really is <u>justice</u>.

_____1_____ c. Anwar Khalil was convicted 18 months ago for an ATM robbery. *Metro 5 News* anchor Katherine Morrison reports that the case was based on <u>circumstantial evidence</u>.

_____ d. A closed-circuit video camera recorded the robbery. Khalil looked like the man on the video. The <u>victim</u> also identified Khalil in a lineup. Because of new evidence, Khalil will be given a new trial.

_____ e. In her opening statement at the trial, Marilyn Corbin, Khalil's lawyer, tells the jury about the new evidence. Khalil has an <u>alibi</u> that will prove that he is innocent.

Write the underlined words in the paragraphs next to their definitions below.

1. proof that someone was not where a crime happened and is not guilty of the crime _____

2. system by which people are judged in courts of law and criminals are punished _____

3. someone affected by a crime _____

4. official decision by a jury in a court of law about whether someone is guilty _____ *verdict* _____

5. evidence that appears believable but cannot be proven _____

6. clears a person of a charge by declaring him or her not guilty _____

🔔 🔔 🔔 **Imagine that Carla Castillo interviews Anwar Khalil after the trial. Role-play with someone. Your partner is Carla. You are Anwar Khalil.**

> **How do you feel about the jury's verdict?**

> **I feel wonderful.**

CARLA: Why did this jury find you innocent?

ANWAR KHALIL:

CARLA: How did the legal system protect your rights?

ANWAR KHALIL:

CARLA: What advice would you give to other people charged with a crime?

ANWAR KHALIL:

The Police Officers' Story

🔔 **Read what people said. Look at the pictures. Complete the chart.**

Sandra Baker
Police officer

Brenda
Diane Clayton's sister

Diane Clayton
Community Relations

Frankie
Accused drug dealer

Phil Genelli
Police officer

Edward Reilly
Mayor

Dave Kinnard
Chief of Police

Derek Powell
Mayor's Assistant

What People Said	Who Said It	To Whom
1. "I went up to his room, and he was just lying there. He was barely breathing."	*Brenda*	*Diane Clayton*
2. "I don't have enough cops to cover the areas where the drugs are sold."		
3. "You are under arrest for possession of narcotics."		
4. "It wasn't a clean search. I don't want to perjure myself."		
5. "You want to catch the bad guys . . . Sometimes you have to bend the rules a little."		

🔔 🔔 **Put the paragraphs in order. Number them 1 to 6.**

_____ a. In court, Genelli <u>testifies</u> that the brown paper bag was on the back seat of the car. He could see small plastic bags inside the brown bag. Then Officer Baker testifies. She admits that the paper bag was under the driver's seat.

___*1*___ b. City officials are worried about drug dealers, especially around schools. It is difficult to catch these dealers with <u>evidence</u> that can be used in court. Police officers Genelli and Baker watch a car circling the high school from their unmarked police car.

_____ c. The case is dismissed because due process procedures in gathering evidence were not followed.

_____ d. Frankie and Nick's attorney meets with Assistant District Attorney Marty Siegel. Their attorney wants the <u>charges</u> dropped. He says that the paper bag was under the seat and not clearly visible. This is an <u>illegal search</u>.

_____ e. Baker talks with Genelli about the upcoming trial. She is worried about testifying. She says she doesn't want to commit <u>perjury</u>.

_____ f. The police officers, suspicious of the car, question the two men when they park. Genelli looks around the car while Baker checks the driver's record. When Genelli finds a brown paper bag containing white powder, he <u>arrests</u> the men.

Write the underlined words in the paragraphs next to their definitions below.

1. something legally submitted to a court of law to determine the truth

   _____

2. searching a person's home, car, or other property without obtaining permission or without having a warrant signed by a judge

   _____

3. official statements accusing someone of a crime _____

4. crime of deliberately giving false, misleading, or incomplete testimony under oath

   _____

5. takes or keeps in custody by authority of law _____

6. gives information under oath in a court of law _____*testifies*_____

🔔 🔔 🔔 **Imagine that Officer Genelli talks to Officer Baker after the trial. Role-play with someone. Your partner is Officer Genelli. You are Officer Baker.**

Why did you contradict my testimony?

In a court of law, I must tell the truth.

OFFICER GENELLI: I'm your partner. We're supposed to support each other, no matter what.

OFFICER BAKER:

OFFICER GENELLI: Your actions freed two drug dealers!

OFFICER BAKER:

OFFICER GENELLI: You don't know anything about law enforcement.

OFFICER BAKER:

Remember Turning Points

🔔 **Write T (True) or F (False) next to each statement.**

___T___ 1. The Fifth Amendment to the Constitution protects people from unfair and unreasonable treatment by the federal government.

_____ 2. The Constitution does not address the question of whether or not state governments must also treat people fairly.

_____ 3. Due process is a fair and reasonable plan for paying back borrowed money.

_____ 4. Under due process, government cannot pass laws that interfere with what people believe, the friends they choose, or where they live.

_____ 5. Due process applies to everyone except people charged with committing a serious crime.

🔔 🔔 **Read the phrases on the right. Write each phrase in one of the four spaces in the column where it belongs.**

Due Process	
Content of Laws (What does due process protect?)	**Procedures** (How does due process provide fair treatment?)
1. *what people believe*	1.
2.	2.
3.	3.
4.	4.

- what people believe

- trying people charged with crimes

- enforcing the law

- where people choose to live

- the kind of work people do

- investigating crimes

- the friends people choose

- conducting hearings

For each characteristic of due process on the left, write an example on the right.

Due Process	
Characteristics	Examples
1. Laws cannot interfere with what people believe.	*People are free to worship whatever god they choose, or no god at all.*
2. Laws cannot interfere with the kind of work people do.	
3. Laws cannot interfere with where people choose to live.	
4. Laws cannot interfere with the friends people choose.	
5. Police must use fair methods in investigating crime and enforcing the law.	
6. Courts must use fair methods in conducting hearings and trying people charged with crimes.	

Making Connections

Read the quote below. Think about the questions. Share your answers with someone.

> The police must use fair methods in investigating crimes, and the courts must use fair procedures in trying people charged with crimes.

1. Whom did the police investigate in each story?

2. What were the charges against the suspect in each story?

1. What methods did the police use to investigate each case?

2. What procedures did the courts use in trying each case?

1. What should the police do differently next time about collecting evidence or questioning witnesses in Anwar Khalil's story?

2. What should they do differently in the police officers' story?

What is due process of law?

It is difficult to define **due process of law** exactly. The closest meaning is *the right to be treated fairly by government.* This meaning is applied in two important ways.

▶ *Due process* means that the content of laws that legislatures pass must be fair and reasonable. Congress and the state legislatures cannot pass laws that place unfair or unreasonable limitations on a person's right to life, liberty, or property. This is known as **substantive due process**.

▶ *Due process* also means that the procedures, or methods, used to conduct hearings and enforce the law must be fair and reasonable. All branches of federal and state government must use fair procedures when they carry out their responsibilities. This is known as **procedural due process**.

What does the U.S. Constitution say about due process?

The words *due process of law* were not part of the original **Constitution**. They were added when the first ten amendments, called the **Bill of Rights**, were approved. Before the Bill of Rights was ratified, all the original state constitutions used the phrase "law of the land" to refer to procedural due process.

The due process clause is found in two places in the Constitution—in the Fifth **Amendment** of the Bill of Rights, ratified in 1791, and in the Fourteenth Amendment, ratified in 1868.

The Fifth Amendment was designed to protect people from unfair and unreasonable treatment by the federal government. It says, *No person shall be deprived of life, liberty, or property, without due process of law.*

The Fourteenth Amendment protects people from unfair and unreasonable treatment by state governments. Section I states, . . . *nor shall any State deprive any person of life, liberty, or property, without due process of law.* Over the years, the Supreme Court has interpreted this to mean that almost all the protections in the Bill of Rights apply to actions of state governments as well as to actions of the federal government.

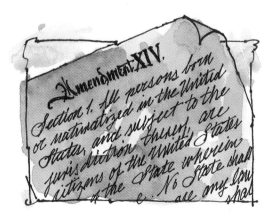

During the twentieth century, the United States Supreme Court has used these two due process clauses to strengthen individual rights and to prevent government from making laws or taking actions that interfere with certain areas of your life. Government cannot interfere with what you believe, the friends you choose, the kind of work you do, or where you travel.

The Supreme Court has overturned laws that give government unfair control over personal freedoms. For example, in 1965, in *Griswold v. Connecticut,* the Court ruled that the due process clause protects the privacy of married couples. For this reason, a state law cannot outlaw the use of contraceptives by married couples.

What happens when the rights of the individual conflict with the rights of society?

Government is responsible for protecting the rights of all people, even people who have broken the law and **endangered** the lives, liberty, or property of others. In the United States, people who are accused of breaking a law are presumed innocent unless they are found guilty by a jury of their **peers**. There are strict rules about the following:

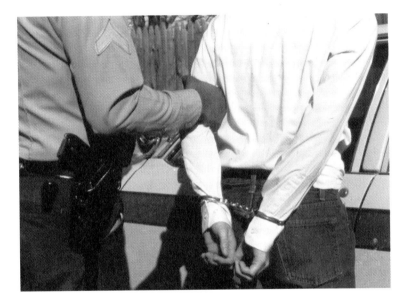

► what evidence can be used, and how it can be obtained
► what testimony is relevant, and how it can be challenged

It is difficult to balance these two responsibilities. People in government and the court system face this challenge every day. In spite of this difficulty, due process is among the most important protections of a constitutional democracy.

Use information in the reading on pages 10 and 11 to complete the sentences. Underline or highlight the sentence in the reading that supports your answer. Then write the sentence in the space below the choices.

1. Due process requires all laws to be
   a. clear and specific.
   b. fair and reasonable.
   c. focused on process.

Due process means that the content of laws that legislatures pass must be fair and reasonable.

2. The words *due process of law* appear in
   a. the original Constitution.
   b. all the amendments.
   c. the Bill of Rights.

3. The Fifth Amendment protects people from unfair treatment by
   a. the federal government.
   b. state governments.
   c. city governments.

4. The U.S. government must protect the due process rights of
   a. all people who break the law.
   b. only people who obey the law.
   c. some people who break the law.

Complete the sentences. Use your own words.

1. *Procedural due process* means that _____

_____

2. In a trial, the rules of due process control _____

_____

_____

Think about the questions. Share your answers with someone.

1. How have the Fifth and Fourteenth Amendments influenced Supreme Court decisions?

2. What individual freedoms does due process give you?

Pick Your Project

Do one or more of the following activities. Share your work with someone.

Community Matters: Interact!

It is often difficult for people to understand the importance of due process of law unless they have had their rights violated. Interview three people who have watched "Rules of the Game." Ask them these questions and take notes.

▶ Do you think that the rules of due process are too easy on people suspected of committing a crime? In what way?

▶ How would you change the process?

▶ Imagine that you were accused of a crime you didn't commit. How would you feel about due process then?

In the News: Get the Facts!

Collect at least two articles from newspapers or news magazines about a law being challenged in court because some people feel it is unfair (substantive due process). Make a chart like the one below.

Source of Information	Issue	Argument
Morning Sentinel February 3	**Affirmative action**	**Affirmative action policies discriminate against people who are not members of a minority group.**
The People's Voice February 4	**Affirmative action**	**Affirmative action is the only way to correct past injustices. The policies eventually create a stronger, more united nation.**

If you were a judge, what decision would you make about the law? Why?

Creative Works: React!

Draw at least three scenes that show what life might be like without due process of law.

Inside Information

Here Comes the Judge!

The judicial branch of government interprets the law and settles disagreements between individuals and the government. First complete the sentences. Then circle the missing words in the puzzle. Some of this information was provided in the first seven units of *On Common Ground*. The words are written across, up and down, or diagonally. If you don't know an answer, look back through earlier units or ask a friend.

A	S	P	C	O	N	S	T	I	T	U	T	I	O	N
R	I	P	L	F	A	T	O	R	H	C	B	L	I	U
K	J	O	P	T	O	M	E	E	I	G	H	T	P	G
S	U	P	R	E	M	E	D	J	Q	U	E	I	N	Y
H	S	R	E	L	V	X	C	G	T	F	M	B	E	S
A	T	L	S	F	E	R	N	R	P	D	C	B	E	F
L	I	M	I	H	A	P	P	E	A	L	S	T	T	Q
T	C	P	D	N	C	L	R	T	U	G	A	F	H	U
R	E	M	E	A	Q	R	D	I	E	T	B	V	A	S
T	S	E	N	A	T	E	L	R	S	C	A	R	E	S
I	T	N	T	T	L	N	A	E	T	C	U	S	R	A

1. The highest court in the land is called the **Supreme** Court.

2. The judges who serve on this court are called _____.

3. The person who heads this group of judges is the _____ justice.

4. There are _____ judges who also serve as associates.

5. Members of the court are appointed by the _____ and confirmed by the _____.

6. They serve on the court until they _____ or _____.

7. The highest court handles a limited number of _____ that have already gone through the lower courts.

8. It interprets the _____ and settles disputes between _____.

Now check your progress on Unit 8, *Rules of the Game.* **Turn to page 142.**

9 Sticks and Stones, Part 1

The U.S. criminal justice system protects victims and also people accused of crimes.

In this episode, an immigrant store owner is the victim of a crime.

What can the store owner do? What can the teenager accused of the crime do?

Preview the Story

Look at the pictures. Think about these questions. Share your ideas with someone.

What do you see?

What are these people thinking? What are they feeling?

What do you think will happen?

Preview Turning Points

The Constitution of the United States says that no one should be arrested or convicted of a crime unless rules of due process are followed. Due process is the right to be treated fairly by government.

Think about the ideas above as you look at the pictures.

Think about these questions. Share your answers with someone.

What examples of unfair treatment do you see?

Think of someone who was charged with a crime. What steps were followed before the person was charged?

Why are due process procedures important in a democracy?

Remember the Story

Read what people said. Look at the pictures. Complete the chart.

Mr. Hadim

Lawrence Hamilton
Defense Attorney

Scooter Harrison

Mrs. Jensen

Rick Jensen

Mike Murdock
Detective

Edward Tarkowitz
Store owner

What People Said	Who Said It	To Whom
1. "This is not the first time you have stolen from me; but this time you are not leaving until you pay."	Edward Tarkowitz	Rick Jensen
2. "What are you doing? Are you crazy? You said you were just going to scare him."		
3. "You just keep your mouth shut, and this whole thing will blow over."		
4. "Mr. Jensen has agreed to let Rick be questioned so that this whole matter can be cleared up."		
5. "Who would believe an immigrant's word against a boy from a rich family?"		
6. "I promise we'll just take a quick look, and we'll be out before you know it."		

Put the paragraphs in order. Number them 1 to 5.

_____ a. The detectives find a ring with a missing stone at Jensen's house. The stone they found at the crime scene fits the ring. The detectives go to the high school football field. They arrest Rick and read him his Miranda rights.

_____ b. After Mr. Tarkowitz points out Rick Jensen as his attacker, Detectives Burrows and Murdock take Jensen in for questioning. His father and an attorney come with him. The attorney asks, "Are you charging Rick with assault and battery? You'd better have solid evidence."

_____1_____ c. Two high school football players, Rick and Scooter, stop by a convenience store and <u>harass</u> its owner, Edward Tarkowitz. When Rick steals candy and hides it in his pocket, Mr. Tarkowitz tries to make him pay for it. That night Rick waits behind the store for Mr. Tarkowitz and beats him unconscious.

_____5_____ d. Detective Murdock stops the questioning. He wants to charge Rick, but he needs more than Tarkowitz's testimony to <u>convict</u> him. Rick's attorney, Mr. Hamilton, is very good in court. After Hamilton <u>cross-examines</u> Tarkowitz, the jury may not believe him.

_____3_____ e. The owner of the business next door finds Mr. Tarkowitz lying on the ground. An ambulance and some detectives come to the crime scene. The detectives look for evidence at the scene and find a small colored stone.

Write the underlined words in the paragraphs next to their definitions below.

1. violent attack intended to hurt someone   _____

2. to annoy or torment someone   _____

3. information given by the police to the accused during the arrest procedure   _____*Miranda rights*_____

4. to find someone guilty of a crime in a court of law   _____

5. asks a witness questions about something the witness testified to under oath in a court of law   _____

🔔 🔔 🔔 **Imagine that Mr. Hadim, the owner of the business next to the convenience store, talks to Edward Tarkowitz after Jensen is arrested. Role-play with someone. Your partner is Mr. Hadim. You are Edward Tarkowitz.**

> Why didn't you identify Jensen at first?

> I was afraid he would hurt me or a member of my family.

MR. HADIM: Why did you change your mind?

EDWARD TARKOWITZ:

MR. HADIM: What will you do at the trial?

EDWARD TARKOWITZ:

MR. HADIM: You are an immigrant. Jensen's family is rich. What makes you think that the trial can be fair?

EDWARD TARKOWITZ:

Remember Turning Points

🔔 **Write *T (True)* or *F (False)* next to each statement.**

___F___ 1. The purpose of the criminal justice system is to protect victims of a crime, not people charged with committing a crime.

___F___ 2. The Framers of the Constitution were not concerned with the rights of the accused.

___T___ 3. The Constitution of the United States says that no one can be detained or arrested without good reason.

___T___ 4. Due process procedures are designed to be fair and reasonable to people convicted of a crime.

___F___ 5. Constitutional rights to due process depend upon the color of a person's skin and country of birth.

🔔🔔 **Read the phrases in the box. Place the number of the phrase in the correct circle to show what law enforcement officials are expected to do and what they cannot do under due process.**

1. arrest people because they disagree with the government	4. convict people easily
2. protect people accused of crimes	5. convict people without a trial
3. follow established procedures for sentencing people convicted of crimes	6. sentence people convicted of crimes

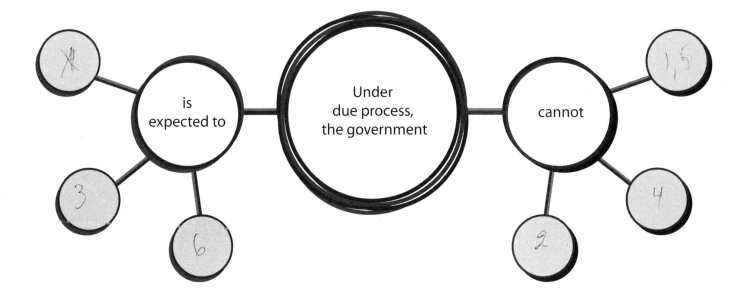

Read the words on the left that describe due process. For each concept, give an example from the story, or from something you have heard or read, that illustrates what the concept means.

Due Process	Example
1. protects people suspected of crimes	*The detectives cannot charge Rick Jensen without solid evidence.*
2. protects people charged with crimes	
3. protects people on trial for crimes	

Making Connections

Read the quote below. Think about the questions. Share your answers with someone.

> In recent years, there has been greater emphasis on assisting all victims of crime. At the same time, the Constitution makes it clear that law enforcement officials must also protect the rights of people who are accused of crimes.

In this story, who is accused of a crime?

Who is the victim?

Who are the law enforcement officials?

What was the crime?

When was the accused charged with the crime?

Did the law enforcement officials protect the rights of the accused? If so, how?

Did they violate any of the rights of the accused? If so, how?

How does the Constitution protect the rights of people accused of crimes?

Why did the Founders of this country want to protect the rights of people accused of breaking the law? During the colonial period, the government accused many innocent people of crimes and put them in jail. In some cases, they were not given a **trial** and did not have the right to **appeal**. To allow a government to have such powers puts everyone at risk.

In the United States, people accused of crimes are assumed to be "**innocent** until proven **guilty**." In criminal cases, the government must prove the guilt of the accused beyond a **reasonable doubt**. In contrast, defendants do not have to prove their innocence. The Constitution does not actually say this, but this idea is basic to due process.

Due process is the right to be treated fairly by government. In the criminal justice system, this means that government must follow certain procedures when it investigates, tries, or punishes someone for a crime. It is difficult to understand how important this concept is unless you have had your rights violated.

Many due process rights are specifically mentioned in the Constitution.

WRIT OF HABEAS CORPUS
(Article I, Section 9)

People cannot be held in jail unless they are charged with a crime and given a trial. A Writ of Habeas Corpus is a paper that orders the police to bring the prisoner to court and to prove they have enough evidence to charge the person with a crime. If the court decides there is not enough evidence, the prisoner must be released.

TRIAL BY JURY
(Article 3, Section 3, and the Sixth Amendment)

The Constitution guarantees a trial by jury for people accused of committing a crime.

LIMITS ON SEARCH AND SEIZURE
(Fourth Amendment)

People have a basic right to privacy. People cannot be searched or their property taken without a **warrant**.

LIMITS ON CRIMINAL CHARGES
(Fifth Amendment)

People cannot be tried twice for the same **offense** and cannot be forced to testify against themselves.

RIGHT TO A FAIR TRIAL
(Sixth Amendment)

A fair trial, as defined by the Constitution, includes the following:

- ▶ the right to know the charges against you
- ▶ the right to a **speedy and public trial**
- ▶ the right to an **impartial** jury
- ▶ the right to be defended by legal **counsel**
- ▶ the right to force witnesses to appear in court
- ▶ the right to cross-examine witnesses

TRIAL BY JURY FOR CIVIL CASES
(Seventh Amendment)

A person involved in a **lawsuit** against another person or company can ask for a trial by jury.

BAIL, FINES, AND PUNISHMENT
(Eighth Amendment)

The **bail** for people accused of a crime, and the **fines** and **sentences** for people convicted of a crime, must be fair and reasonable.

Use information in the reading on pages 22 and 23 to complete the sentences. Underline or highlight the sentence in the reading that supports your answer. Then write the sentence in the space below the choices.

1. In the United States, people suspected of committing crimes are
   a. guilty when the police make the arrest.
   b. guilty when a court proves their guilt.
   c. innocent until they commit another crime.

   In the United States, people accused of crimes are assumed to be "innocent until proven guilty."

2. The right to due process means that
   a. guilty people get shorter sentences.
   b. people who break the laws lose their rights.
   c. government should be fair to all people.

3. Under the U.S. Constitution, the courts can jail a person who
   a. criticizes the government.
   b. is found innocent in a trial.
   c. is charged with a crime.

4. The U.S. government
   a. needs a warrant to search public property.
   b. needs a warrant to search private property.
   c. has no power to search private property.

Complete the sentences. Use your own words.

1. The men who wrote the Constitution gave rights to people accused of crimes because

   _____

   _____

2. Three rights of a person on trial for a crime are _____

   _____

Think about the questions. Share your answers with someone.

1. What are some examples of due process in the U.S. courts?

2. Is it fair to protect the rights of someone accused of a crime? Why or why not?

Pick Your Project

Do one or more of the following activities. Share your ideas with someone.

Community Matters: Interact!

In most communities, the police have educational programs about crime prevention and about what to do if you are a victim of a crime. Contact your local police department to ask for printed information about these issues:

▶ crime prevention
▶ how crime victims can get help
▶ rights of an accused person in an arrest

In the News: Get the Facts!

Collect information about three different cases in which a person charged with a crime claims his or her due process rights were violated. The source of the information can be news broadcasts or articles in newspapers or news magazines. Make a chart like the one below.

Name of Accused and Source	Due Process Right	Issue	Constitutional Link
David Kim The Front Page	Right to a speedy and public trial	Trial date has not been set. Crime he's charged with occurred 18 months ago.	Sixth Amendment

Think about the facts that are presented and what you've learned in this unit. What do you think will happen in each of the cases you've listed?

Creative Works: React!

In the story, Mr. Hadim is quite upset about his friend, Mr. Tarkowitz, and the beating he has suffered. He feels that this crime occurred, in part, because Mr. Tarkowitz is an immigrant. He does not understand why criminals are protected by due process procedures.

Write a poem, tell a story, or draw a picture to help victims of crime understand why the due process procedures are important.

Inside Information

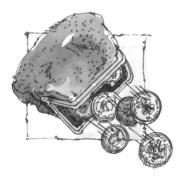

Coins of the Realm

The United States, like many countries, honors its heroes by putting their pictures on coins and bills. Find out whose picture is on each of these coins and bills and why the person was selected for recognition. If you don't know some of the answers, ask a friend or check at the library or a bank.

Coin or bill	Whose picture is on it?	Why was each person honored?
penny		
nickel		
dime		*He became president during the Great Depression, and he led the country during World War II.*
quarter		
half-dollar		
one-dollar bill		
five-dollar bill		
ten-dollar bill	*Alexander Hamilton*	
twenty-dollar bill		
fifty-dollar bill		
one-hundred dollar bill		

Now check your progress on Unit 9, *Sticks and Stones, Part 1.* Turn to page 144.

10 Sticks and Stones, Part 2

The purpose of a court trial in the United States is to find the truth based on evidence.

In this episode, lawyers for the state and the accused present their cases at a trial.

What steps are followed in a trial?

Preview the Story

Look at the pictures. Think about these questions. Share your ideas with someone.

What do you see?

What are these people thinking? What are they feeling?

What do you think will happen?

Preview Turning Points

In the United States, most trials have two opposing sides. Each side tries to prove its case before an impartial jury. The purpose of the trial is to determine whether the defendant is guilty of the charges.

Think about the ideas above as you look at the pictures.

Think about these questions. Share your answers with someone.

These pictures are from a trial in the United States. What do you think is happening?

In other countries you know about, what happens when someone is accused of a crime?

What do these differences tell you about the kind of government each country has?

Remember the Story

Read what people said. Look at the pictures. Complete the chart.

Phil Burrows
Detective

Lawrence Hamilton
Defense Attorney

Scooter Harrison

Mayor Reilly

Judge

Jury

Marty Siegel
Assistant District Attorney

What People Said	Who Said It	To Whom
1. "We will prove that this is an unfortunate case of mistaken identity."	*Lawrence Hamilton*	*Jury*
2. "It was in a partially opened drawer in plain sight, so we didn't need a warrant."		
3. "I'm going to rule the ring, and any mention of the ring, inadmissible as evidence."		
4. "I'm afraid of how some people might react if they believe that equal justice is more equal for some than for others."		
5. "I tried to stop him!"		

Put the paragraphs in order. Number them 1 to 5.

_____ a. The next <u>witness</u> to be called is a jeweler. The defense attorney objects. He says that the ring which will be introduced as evidence was obtained illegally. He doesn't want the <u>jury</u> to hear the jeweler's testimony about the ring.

_____ b. Finally, Scooter testifies. At first, he says that Rick was studying with him at the time of the beating. But when Assistant District Attorney Siegel shows Scooter photos of Tarkowitz right after the beating and continues to ask him questions, Scooter admits that he tried to stop Jensen.

_____ c. When the detectives found the ring, they didn't have a <u>search warrant</u>. The judge rules the ring <u>inadmissible</u> as evidence.

_____ d. The first witness for the <u>prosecution</u> is Mr. Lee, the crime lab technician. He testifies that the shoe found in Rick's home matches prints found at the crime scene. In his cross examination, Mr. Hamilton, attorney for the <u>defense</u>, demonstrates that many shoes of the same make and size are sold each year. The lab technician admits that he can't be sure the print is Rick's.

_**1**_ e. Convenience store owner Edward Tarkowitz says that Rick Jensen beat him. Detectives Murdock and Burrows question Rick's friend Scooter. Scooter says that he didn't have anything to do with the beating. Murdock warns Scooter, "You know what happens if you lie in court? They call it perjury."

Write the underlined words in the paragraphs next to their definitions below.

1. lawyers representing the person accused of a crime in a court of law

   _____

2. group of people who listen to details of a case in a court of law and decide whether the accused is innocent or guilty

   _____

3. lawyers representing the state in a case against a person charged with a crime

   _____

4. order by a judge that authorizes a police officer to search a specific place

   _____

5. person called to give evidence in a court

   _____ *witness* _____

6. not acceptable; not allowed

   _____

🔔 🔔 🔔 **Imagine that Derek Powell talks to Assistant District Attorney Marty Siegel. Role-play with someone. Your partner is Derek Powell. You are Marty Siegel.**

Why did you try to introduce the ring as evidence?

The detectives said that they were following procedures when they found the ring in Rick's bedroom.

DEREK POWELL: What made Scooter tell the truth on the witness stand?

MARTY SIEGEL:

DEREK POWELL: What do you think the jury will decide?

MARTY SIEGEL:

DEREK POWELL: What if Scooter hadn't told the truth?

MARTY SIEGEL:

Remember Turning Points

Write **T (True)** or **F (False)** next to each statement.

___F___ 1. In most legal cases tried in the United States, there are three opposing parties: the prosecution, the defense, and the jury.

_____ 2. The purpose of a trial is to determine the truth, based on evidence.

_____ 3. Citizens called to serve on a jury are questioned only by the defense attorney to make sure that the prosecution does not have an unfair advantage.

_____ 4. The person accused of the crime must be present in the courtroom and must testify on his or her own behalf.

_____ 5. If the suspect is found guilty, the prosecuting and defense attorneys negotiate a fair sentence.

Compare the roles of prosecuting and defense attorneys. Put the number of the phrase in the section of the circle diagram where it belongs. Put a check by each word or phrase after you use it.

1. call witnesses ✓	5. examine evidence against the defendant
2. collect evidence against defendant ✓	6. may object to how evidence was collected
3. cross-examine witnesses for the defense	7. make closing arguments
4. cross-examine witnesses for the prosecution	8. make opening statements
	9. question citizens called to serve on the jury

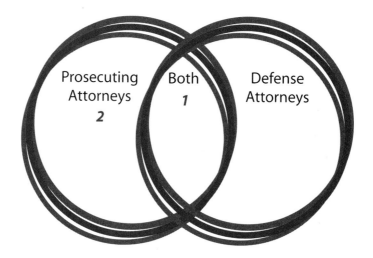

Prosecuting Attorneys
2

Both
1

Defense Attorneys

🔔 🔔 🔔 Define in your own words the roles of people involved in a trial.

People	Roles
1. attorneys	• *collect evidence* • *question potential jurors* • *make opening statements* • *call witnesses* • *cross-examine witnesses called by the opposing side* • *make closing arguments*
2. defendant	• • •
3. jury	• • •
4. judge	• • •

Making Connections

Read the quote below. Think about the questions. Share your answers with someone.

> In most legal cases tried in the United States, there are two opposing parties: the prosecution and the defense. The purpose of the trial is to determine the truth, based on evidence. The defense attorney may object to how certain pieces of evidence were obtained. The judge determines whether the evidence can be used.

🔔 In this story, who is the prosecuting attorney? Who is the defense attorney?

🔔 🔔 What were two pieces of evidence? What did the judge do about some of the evidence? Why?

🔔 🔔 🔔 Was the judge impartial? Give examples from the story to show whether his treatment of both sides was fair.

The purpose of the U.S. criminal justice system is to find and punish people who have committed crimes. To protect the people's rights, the government must follow specific steps before deciding whether or not a person is guilty.

Arresting a suspect	The police have **probable cause**—good reason—to believe that a **suspect**—we will call him Albert Suspect—committed a crime. During the arrest procedure, the officers must tell Mr. Suspect that he has the right to remain silent and to have a lawyer present when he is questioned. This is called the **Miranda warning**.
Booking the suspect	After the arrest, the police take Suspect to a police station and **book** him. They record his name, the time of the arrest, and the charges against him. Mr. Suspect has the right to telephone an attorney, or someone else, before he is jailed.
Deciding which court	There are different levels of courts in the United States: municipal, state, and federal. The charges against Mr. Suspect influence the choice of court that will handle his case. Murder cases, for example, are usually tried in a state court.
Assigning a prosecutor	A **prosecuting attorney** is assigned to Mr. Suspect's case. The prosecutor reviews the government's case against Mr. Suspect. If the prosecutor decides the case is too weak, he will drop the charges and release Suspect.
Holding the preliminary hearing	At the preliminary hearing, the prosecutor must convince the judge that a crime has been committed and that there is enough evidence against the defendant to proceed. The judge can dismiss the case if there is not probable cause to believe Suspect committed the crime.
Appointing a defense attorney	If the crime could lead to jail or a prison sentence, Mr. Suspect has the right to an attorney. If he cannot pay for an attorney, the court will appoint a **defense attorney**.
Setting bail	At this first appearance, the judge may set bail—money that the defendant gives the court as a promise that he will return for the trial. If Mr. Suspect doesn't return, the court keeps the bail, and a warrant is issued for his arrest. The judge may decide not to grant bail if the defendant is considered dangerous to society. In that case, the defendant must stay in jail until the trial.

Entering a plea	When Mr. Suspect is officially charged with the crime, he enters a plea of guilty or not guilty. If he pleads guilty, no trial is needed. If he pleads not guilty, preparation for the trial continues.
Examining the evidence	Before the trial begins, the defense attorney examines the evidence against the client. The attorney may object to how the police acquired the evidence and ask that it not be admitted in court. If the judge decides in favor of the defense, the prosecutor may not have enough evidence to continue the case.
Offering to plea bargain	If the evidence against Mr. Suspect is strong, the defense attorney may advise his client to **plea bargain**—to plead guilty in exchange for a less serious charge or a shorter sentence. The government saves the cost of a trial, and the defendant's punishment is not as severe.
Selecting a jury	In the United States, Albert Suspect has the right to a trial before a jury of his peers. Serving as jurors, when asked, is a responsibility of citizens. The prosecuting attorney and the defense attorney question many potential jurors before they agree on 12 people who will be fair and impartial.
Conducting the trial	The purpose of the trial is to decide on the truth, based on the evidence. Is Mr. Suspect guilty or not guilty of the charges against him? Due process specifies that the trial must be speedy and public. Albert Suspect has the right to call witnesses and to question witnesses called by the prosecution. He has the right to be in the courtroom, but he does not have to answer questions.
Reaching a verdict	After closing arguments, the judge gives directions to the jury and asks them to make their decision. Is the defendant guilty "beyond a reasonable doubt"? They must decide. If the jury finds Mr. Suspect not guilty, he will be released. If the jury finds Mr. Suspect guilty, the final step is to decide how he will be punished.
Determining the sentence	The law establishes both maximum and minimum sentences for most crimes. In some capital crimes, the jury has a role in sentencing. The judge considers the seriousness of the crime, as well as Mr. Suspect's criminal record, age, and attitude in deciding his punishment—the sentence.

Use information in the reading on pages 34 and 35 to complete the sentences. Underline or highlight the sentence in the reading that supports your answer. Then write the sentence in the space below the choices.

1. After the police book Mr. Suspect, he
   a. goes to a jail cell immediately.
   b. can leave the police station.
   c. has the right to call someone.

   Mr. Suspect has the right to telephone an attorney, or someone else, before he is jailed.

2. Before the trial, Albert Suspect may agree to plead guilty in order to receive
   a. special treatment in a trial.
   b. help from a defense attorney.
   c. a shorter prison sentence.

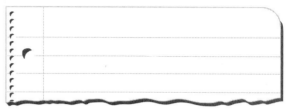

3. If Suspect doesn't appear for trial, the
   a. jury has to find him not guilty.
   b. court keeps his bail money and issues a warrant for his arrest.
   c. judge puts his attorney in jail and does not grant bail.

4. At a preliminary hearing, the judge can stop a case if the
   a. prosecutor does not have enough evidence.
   b. defendant is considered dangerous to society.
   c. defendant does not have enough money for bail.

Complete the sentences. Use your own words.

1. The Miranda warning says _____

   _____

2. *Probable cause* means _____

   _____

Think about the questions. Share your answers with someone.

1. Why do some cases never go to trial?

2. How are the rights of people accused of crimes sometimes violated?

Pick Your Project

Do one or more of the following activities. Share your work with someone.

Community Matters: Interact!

Visit a court to watch the legal system in progress. Before you visit, call the courthouse for the schedule of jury trials and information on when the public can watch a trial.

In the courtroom, look for these people:

▶ the defendant
▶ the defense attorney
▶ the prosecuting attorney
▶ the jury
▶ the judge

Find answers to these questions and take notes:

▶ What was the crime?
▶ What evidence was presented?
▶ Was there a verdict? If so, what was it?

In the News: Get the Facts!

Collect at least three articles or reports about a controversial trial or trials. Skim the articles to find contrasting accounts of the same event or different opinions about the same crime. Make and fill out a chart like the one below.

Source and Date	Contrasting Accounts or Opinions
Evening Dispatch *May 15*	*Mary Brown, 42, murders sleeping husband, Joe Brown, 45, president of major company and respected city leader.*
Afternoon Gazette *May 16*	*Mary Brown physically abused by husband. Suffered third broken arm. Afraid husband would kill her; shoots him in self-defense.*

Compare and contrast the credibility of the accounts or opinions. How do you decide which one is valid? What conclusions can you make about how readers or listeners decide if the news is accurate?

Creative Works: React!

Design a one-page fact sheet for new immigrants on the U.S. legal system. Make sure that the fact sheet is easy to read and has a chart, a graph, or art to make it interesting and easy to understand. Include this information:

▶ rights of the accused in an arrest
▶ local help, or resources, for a person accused of a crime
▶ rights of the defendant in a trial

Inside Information

State the Facts!

It is interesting to learn about individual states. Here's your chance. Answer the questions by putting the number of the item in the correct state on the map or writing the name of the state next to the question. You may not know many of the answers. The fun is in the exploring!

Which state . . .

1. covers the most territory?
2. is smallest in size?
3. has the most people?
4. has the fewest people?
5. is almost surrounded by water?
6. has the most tropical climate?
7. has, on average, the highest elevation?
8. has the most crop, pasture, and forest land?
9. has a major city below sea level?
10. has the largest percentage of coastal, lake, and inland waters?
11. has the most library materials in circulation?
12. has the lowest death rate?
13. is the most densely populated?
14. has the busiest airport, measured by number of departures?
15. has the largest island, without being an island itself?
16. has the largest number of children per household?
17. has the largest percentage of employed women?
18. has the largest number of households with people over 65?

Now check your progress on Unit 10, *Sticks and Stones, Part 2.* Turn to page 146.

11 A House Divided

In a representative democracy, voting is a right and a responsibility.

In this episode, two candidates campaign for a position on the City Council.

What can candidates do to win votes in an election? What can citizens do to be informed voters?

Preview the Story

Look at the pictures. Think about these questions. Share your ideas with someone.

What do you see?

What are these people thinking? What are they feeling?

What do you think will happen?

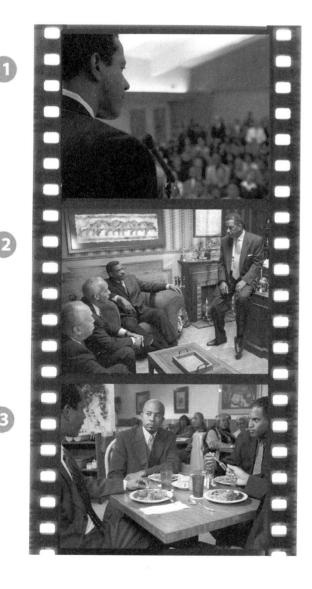

Preview Turning Points

The Constitution provides citizens of the United States with the right to vote and to hold public office.

Think about the idea above as you look at the pictures.

1 1790s

2 1890s

3 1940s

4 1990s

Think about these questions. Share your answers with someone.

Who was allowed to vote in the United States in 1790? In 1890? In 1940? In 1990?

Should anyone not be allowed to vote?

Why is the right to vote essential in a representative democracy?

Remember the Story

Read what people said. Look at the pictures. Complete the chart.

Diane Clayton

Crowd

Thompson supporter

Derek Powell

Mayor Reilly

Nate Thompson
Councilman

Malik Williams
Candidate for councilman

What People Said	Who Said It	To Whom
1. "I'm not about to play by the old rules. I want a community that can rely on itself to grow and prosper."	*Malik Williams*	*Crowd*
2. "There's a system here. And I've learned to work within that system—learned how to play the game."		
3. "You're just so caught up in your 'important position' that you're forgetting you're still a black man."		
4. "I won this office in large part because I had Nate Thompson's support."		
5. "Did you hire me because I was qualified or black?"		
6. "I can tell you it doesn't matter who's running the show. The only one who's going to hold you back is you."		

Put the paragraphs in order. Number them 1 to 5.

___2___ a. Derek Powell agrees with many of Williams' ideas. They meet at a diner. Williams challenges Powell to look at what he's achieved as the Mayor's assistant and asks him to join his <u>campaign</u> team.

___1___ b. Nate Thompson has been a city councilman for ten years. Now, at <u>election</u> time, he wants to be reelected. Thompson has learned to work within the <u>system</u>, and he has the support of the older people in his community.

_____ c. When Derek Powell and Mayor Reilly talk about the <u>candidates</u>, the mayor learns that Powell supports Williams. The mayor knows that Thompson is important to his <u>administration</u> and doubts Powell's loyalty. Powell wonders why Reilly hired him in the first place. He offers to take a <u>leave of absence</u>, but the mayor rejects his offer.

_____ d. Malik Williams, Thompson's <u>challenger</u>, isn't playing by the old rules. He appeals to the younger generation. Thompson's supporters are worried. They have pledged money to the campaign and want to win.

_____ e. As election day nears, the community is divided about which candidate to support. When Diane Clayton sees Derek Powell at church, she says she misses him. His worth does not depend on who wins the election. In the end, Thompson wins the election, and Mayor Reilly asks Powell to return to his job.

Write the underlined words in the paragraphs next to their definitions below.

1. person opposing an incumbent (person currently in office) in an election _challenger_

2. process of selecting public officials _election_

3. executive branch of government _administration_

4. people seeking public office _candidates_

5. organized effort to achieve a candidate's election to public office *campaign*

6. rules, traditions, and government that influence people's lives _system_

7. permission to be absent from duty, employment, or service _leave of absence_

🔔 🔔 🔔 **Imagine that Nate Thompson talks to Derek Powell after the election. Role-play with someone. Your partner is Thompson. You are Powell.**

So, you came back to work for the mayor.

Yes, I just needed some time off.

THOMPSON: I hear that you supported Malik Williams in the election.

POWELL:

THOMPSON: Well, I hope that we can work together now.

POWELL:

THOMPSON: What can we do to unite our community?

POWELL:

Remember Turning Points

🔔 **Match each situation with a category. Write a letter on the line.**

a. women 　　　　 c. white men with property 　　　　 e. laws requiring literacy
　　　　　　　　　　　　　　　　　　　　　　　　　　　　 tests and poll taxes

b. 18- to 21-year olds 　　 d. Fifteenth Amendment

_**c**___ 1. only group allowed to vote in the
　　　　 early days of the United States

_____ 2. what extended the right to vote to all
　　　　 males regardless of race, color, or
　　　　 whether they had been slaves

_____ 3. how some states made it difficult for
　　　　 black men to vote

_____ 4. group that sought the right to vote
　　　　 for years, and finally won it in 1920

_____ 5. before 1970, the group that could not
　　　　 vote for or against the people who
　　　　 were sending them to war

🔔 🔔 **Over the last two centuries in the United States, the right to vote has expanded to include more groups of people. Look at the groups of people in the box below. Show the order in which the five groups gained the right to vote by writing one group on the line for each circle (the most recent group is in the outside circle). Check each one after you use it.**

THE RIGHT TO VOTE

1. _white males with property_

2. _____

3. _____

4. _____

5. _____

- all white males
- black males
- citizens 18 and over
- white males with property ✓
- women

Read the list of historical events in the first column. In the second column, write the group of people who won the right to vote, in part, as a result of that event. In the third column, write the reason.

Event	People Who Won the Right to Vote	Reason
1. Civil War (1860s)	*black males*	*As a result of the North's victory in the Civil War, slaves were freed and black males won the right to vote.*
2. World War I (1914–1918)		
3. Vietnam War (1960s and 1970s)		

Making Connections

Read the quote below. Think about the questions. Share your answers with someone.

The right to vote is a basic ideal in a democracy.

In this story, who is running for office?

Who wants to be reelected?

Who is the challenger?

What are the differences between the two candidates?

What is the result of the election?

Why do you think people voted the way they did?

What mistake did the losing candidate make?

What is the difference between a primary election and a general election?

U.S. **citizens** can vote in two kinds of elections: primary elections and general elections. In a **primary election**, members of **political parties** choose the parties' candidates for office.

In a **general election**, voters make final decisions about candidates and issues. More than 500,000 public offices are filled by general elections, from president of the country to members of town councils.

Who can vote?

To vote in a general election, you must be

- ❏ at least 18 years of age;
- ❏ a citizen of the United States;
- ❏ a resident of the state in which you vote.

However, not everyone who meets these qualifications has the right to vote. For example, people who have been convicted of a **felony** and are in prison or on parole are not allowed to vote. A felony is a crime for which the penalty is a year or more in prison, a fine, or both. Felonies include crimes such as robbery and murder.

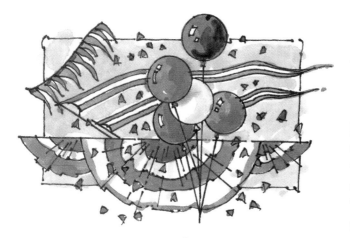

What are the major political parties?

There are two major political parties in the United States—Democrats and Republicans. There are also **third parties**. Although third-party candidates don't often win many votes, they may get enough votes to change the outcome of an election. They also raise issues for the people to think about.

How do you register to vote?

In almost every state, you must register before you vote. Weeks, even months, before an election, cities and towns set up voter registration centers.

Each state has its own rules about voter registration. In some states, registration is permanent. In others, you must reregister every few years. And in still other states, if you fail to vote, you must register again for the next election.

When are elections?

Federal elections are held the Tuesday after the first Monday in November. Most elections for state offices take place at the same time. Primary elections and elections for local officials may be scheduled at any time during the year.

Where do you vote?

People generally vote in neighborhood **polling places**. Election officials will check to see that you are registered before giving you a **ballot**. Ballots are marked in private, small booths. Some polling places have voting machines that also record votes in private.

If you are not able to vote in person on election day, you can ask for an absentee ballot. The ballot must be returned on or before election day.

How can you make your vote count?

Going to the polling place and voting is not hard. But to vote wisely, you must take the time to learn about the candidates and the issues. To be informed, listen to the candidates speak and also read what they have to say. You should learn all you can about their backgrounds, experience, and opinions on the issues.

Organizations like the League of Women Voters will provide you with information about the candidates and the issues on the ballot.

Use information in the reading on pages 46 and 47 to complete the sentences. Underline or highlight the sentence in the reading that supports your answer. Then write the sentence in the space below the choices.

1. In a general election, voters
   a. choose candidates to run for office.
   b. make final decisions about candidates and issues.
   c. only vote for candidates in their party

   In a general election, voters make final decisions about candidates and issues.

2. Before a person can vote, he or she must
   a. live in the United States.
   b. own property.
   c. be a citizen and register to vote.

3. The two major U.S. political parties are the
   a. Democrats and the Republicans.
   b. Progressives and the Independents.
   c. Liberals and the Conservatives.

4. Across the United States, most citizens vote in
   a. neighborhood polling places.
   b. city hall.
   c. the state capital.

Complete the sentences. Use your own words.

1. The qualifications for voting in the United States are _____

   _____

2. Third-party candidates can affect election results because _____

   _____

Think about the questions. Share your answers with someone.

1. What information does a person need to vote wisely?

2. Name at least two groups that are not allowed to vote in the United States. Explain why.

Pick Your Project

Do one or more of the following activities. Share your work with someone.

Community Matters: Interact!

Rules for voting are different in different states. Contact the office of the Registrar of Voters or the Election Commissioner in your community to find out about procedures for voting. Ask questions like the ones below and take notes.

▶ What are the requirements for voting in general elections?
▶ Where can citizens register to vote?
▶ How do people know where to vote at election time?
▶ How can people learn about the candidates?

In the News: Get the Facts!

Collect campaign literature, and listen to speeches and debates by two candidates for the same public office. Compare their positions on at least three major issues, such as taxes, education, and health care. Make and fill out a chart like the one below.

Candidate's Name and Source of Information	Issue	Position
Maria Lopez *Debate, October 23*	*Education*	*Supports a voucher system that would let parents choose their children's school, public or private*
Jane Belenky *Debate, October 23*	*Education*	*Believes a voucher system would mean return to segregated schools. Favors higher standards for public schools. Supports Head Start and Even Start.*

When you complete the chart, study the issues and opposing views. Do the candidates seem consistent on the issues, or do they change their positions for different audiences? Which candidate would you vote for? Why?

Creative Works: React!

Candidates running for public office inform the public about their qualifications and their achievements. Write an ad for radio, television, newspapers, or billboards to convince people to vote for a candidate. Make the ad short but appealing. Use drawings, quotes, facts, or other information to tell people why they should vote for the candidate.

Inside Information

So You Want to be President . . .
or Senator . . . or Representative

Before you begin your campaign, find out more about each elected office and fill in the chart below.

Read the question and answer for the three types of elected offices. Choose your answer from the information in the parentheses.

Question	President	Senator	Representative
1. How many people can hold this office at a given time? (1, 5, 50, 100, 325, 435, 535)	1		
2. If you are elected, how long is your term of office? (2, 4, 6, 8, 10, 12, 14 years)		6 years	
3. How many terms can you serve? (2, 3, 4, 5, 6, no limit)			no limit
4. What is the minimum age for each office? (20, 25, 30, 35, 40, 45, 50)			
5. Must you have been born in the United States? (yes, no)			
6. Must you be a citizen of the United States? (yes, no)			
7. How long must you have lived in the United States? (3, 5, 7, 9, 10, 12, 14, 16 years)			

Now check your progress on Unit 11, *All the Right Moves.* Turn to page 148.

12 Fall from Grace, Part 1

Government in the United States is by the people and for the people. This type of government is called a democracy.

In this episode, Roberto and other tenants have problems in their apartment building.

In a democracy, what options can tenants use to solve their problems?

Preview the Story

Look at the pictures. Think about these questions. Share your ideas with someone.

🔔   What do you see?

🔔 🔔   What are these people thinking? What are they feeling?

🔔 🔔 🔔   What do you think will happen?

Preview Turning Points

The word *democracy* comes from the Greek language. It means *rule by the people*. The United States government is a representative democracy with roots in the history of Athens, Rome, and England.

Think about the ideas above as you look at the pictures.

Think about these questions. Share your answers with someone.

Where do ideas for government come from?

What other systems of government do you know about?

How can people learn from ancient cultures and from events in history?

Remember the Story

Read what people said. Look at the pictures. Complete the chart.

Carla Castillo

Diane Clayton

Amanda Hathaway
Councilwoman

Jess Holcomb
City Attorney

Steve Richardson
News Producer

Roberto Sanchez

Jenny Tang

TV Audience

What People Said	Who Said It	To Whom
1. "We've had problems getting heat in our apartment building."	**Roberto Sanchez**	**Diane Clayton and Jenny Tang**
2. "It sounds like you have a good reason to file a complaint and get the city involved."		
3. "Some slumlords are worse than others. But they're all bad. You want me to get them all? Tell the mayor we need more help."		
4. "I'm not here tonight as a politician. These are people in my district that I care about."		
5. "I'm talking about a real investigation! Who really owns these buildings? Why don't they get fixed up?"		
6. "If your facts are wrong, this station could be on the losing end of a very expensive lawsuit."		

Put the paragraphs in order. Number them 1 to 6.

_____ a. Soon after Diane talks with Jess Holcomb, there is a fire at the Evergreen Apartments. Reporters question the fire chief. Don't building owners have to <u>comply</u> with safety <u>standards</u>? Why have owners been allowed to escape prosecution?

___1___ b. Roberto Sanchez, a worker in the City Hall cafeteria, is having problems with his apartment. There is no heat, and the building has electrical problems. Diane Clayton thinks the owner is in <u>violation</u> of safety standards.

_____ c. Carla begins her own investigation. She finds out that Amanda Hathaway is part of an investment company that owns the building. She shows Hathaway some <u>documents</u>, but Hathaway has no comment.

_____ d. Carla reports on her investigation on *Metro 5 News*. In response, Hathaway holds a press conference and denies the <u>allegations</u> against her.

_____ e. After the fire, the mayor meets with the city attorney and Councilwoman Hathaway. The Evergreen Apartments are in Ms. Hathaway's district. The city attorney is worried about a lawsuit. The mayor wants to increase <u>penalties</u> against owners who don't comply with safety standards. Hathaway wants the city to buy the old properties.

_____ f. Diane talks with Jess Holcomb about Roberto's apartment. He tells her the city has already investigated the building. They found problems, but they didn't find the owner. He says <u>negligent</u> owners are often hard to find.

Write the underlined words in the paragraphs next to their definitions below.

1. act of breaking a rule or law   _____

2. papers such as formal letters, contracts, records   _____

3. basis against which other things are measured   _____

4. punishment for breaking the law   _____

5. statements offered but not yet proved   _____

6. extremely careless, not responsible   _____

7. to obey a request, order, law, or standard   _____*comply*_____

🔔 🔔 🔔   **Imagine that a reporter interviews Councilwoman Amanda Hathaway. Role-play with someone. Your partner is the reporter. You are Amanda Hathaway.**

> What caused the fire at the Evergreen Apartments?

> The building had outdated wiring.

REPORTER: Who should fix the wiring?

AMANDA HATHAWAY:

REPORTER: Why hasn't the city repaired the apartments?

AMANDA HATHAWAY:

REPORTER: As a councilwoman, what is your responsibility to the tenants?

AMANDA HATHAWAY:

Remember Turning Points

Write *T (True)* or *F (False)* next to each statement.

__F__ 1. In a representative democracy, government serves the country's leaders.

_____ 2. The Athenians believed that citizens, working together, could make better decisions than a king.

_____ 3. The Romans elected senators to represent their point of view and to serve the Roman Empire as a whole.

_____ 4. At state and national levels, a direct democracy is more effective than a representative democracy.

_____ 5. Englishman John Locke maintained that the power of government should be limited to protecting the basic rights of the people.

Many ideas about government that form the foundation for the U.S. political system had their roots in governments that existed hundreds and even thousands of years ago. Match the four concepts of government to their sources.

Building a Strong Foundation

- basic rights

- direct democracy

- limited government

- representative government

1. *direct democracy*
2.
3.
4.

Ancient Athens
Ancient Rome
England (Magna Carta)
England (John Locke)

🔔 🔔 🔔 For each definition, write the concept from p. 56. Then give one example from the U.S. political system.

Definition	Concept	Example
1. citizens meet and vote on all issues	*direct democracy*	*town meetings in small New England towns*
2. people elect others to represent their point of view		
3. rights a government cannot take away		
4. a government whose authority depends on the people		

Making Connections

Read the quote below. Think about the questions. Share your answers with someone.

A representative democracy is based on the belief that government exists to serve the needs of the people . . . not the other way around.

🔔 In this episode, who on the City Council represents the tenants in the Evergreen Apartments?

🔔 🔔 Why is it difficult for government officials to do something about the problems at the Evergreen Apartments? Who else tries to do something about the problems? What does this person find out?

🔔 🔔 🔔 How do you think the problems can be solved?

The beginning of this series focused on the early days of this country and the struggle for independence. Have you ever wondered how the Founders of this country chose a form of government for the new nation?

Many of the colonial leaders were students of history. To create the structure of the new government, they used as models governments from the past that respected the power of the people. Here is a closer look at three models that influenced the Founders.

The Democracy of Ancient Athens

Thousands of years ago, most cities in ancient Greece were ruled by powerful kings, but the city of Athens was different. The people of Athens believed that a government of people working together is more effective than a government of any single ruler. And so they created the world's first **direct democracy**, a form of government in which laws are made by the people themselves.

The citizens of Athens met twice a year to discuss ways to make life better in their city. Many years later, the New England colonies had a similar kind of direct democracy. They held town meetings to talk about local issues and vote on them. In certain parts of the United States, the tradition of town meetings still exists today.

The Representative Government of Rome

State and federal legislatures, as well as many local governments in the United States, are more like the representative government of ancient Rome. Because of the great size of the Roman republic, it was difficult for people to make decisions as a group. Instead, citizens elected representatives, called senators, to take care of the business of government.

In a **representative democracy**, the people still have the power of government. When they vote, they give power to the person they choose. That person represents them and serves their interests.

The English Tradition

For centuries, the people of England had no power. Their lives were controlled by kings. Although some kings were wise and fair, others were tyrants—leaders feared and resented by the people they ruled.

In the early 1200s, English nobles became strong enough to challenge King John. They forced the king to sign the **Magna Carta**—an agreement that gave **basic rights** to the nobility. The agreement did not help most people, but it was an important first step. It was the beginning of the idea that people have rights that government cannot challenge—an important idea in the U.S. Constitution.

Centuries later, the English writer John Locke took this idea even further. He wrote that all people have the right to life, liberty, and property. The best way to protect these rights is for people to form a government and obey its laws.

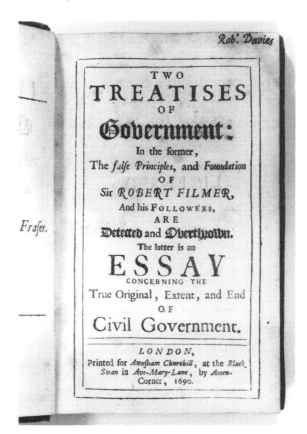

A government formed by the people depends on the **consent of the governed**—the people themselves—for its existence and its power. It is limited because its only purpose is to protect the basic rights of the people. This idea of **limited government** is fundamental to the American political tradition and central to the U.S. Constitution.

Use information in the reading on pages 58 and 59 to complete the sentences. Underline or highlight the sentence in the reading that supports your answer. Then write the sentence in the space below the choices.

1. In the direct democracy of ancient Athens,
   a. people made the laws.
   b. senators made the laws.
   c. the king made the laws.

   And so they created the world's first direct democracy, a form of government in which laws are made by the people themselves.

2. The Congress of the United States is most similar to the
   a. direct democracy of ancient Athens.
   b. representative government of Rome.
   c. English monarchy of the 1200s.

3. The Magna Carta gave
   a. new powers to the English king.
   b. basic rights to the English nobility.
   c. more land to the English peasants.

4. John Locke believed that
   a. all people have the right to life and liberty, but not to property.
   b. government depends on the consent of the people.
   c. the best way to protect people's rights is to eliminate government.

Complete the sentences. Use your own words.

1. In a representative government, people hold power because _____

   _____

2. One idea that the colonial leaders took from the English tradition is _____

   _____

Think about the questions. Share your answers with someone.

1. How is the power of government limited in the United States?

2. How do elected officials represent your interests?

Pick Your Project

Do one or more of the following activities. Share your work with someone.

Community Matters: Interact!

Contact your city council representative about an issue in your neighborhood (housing, traffic, crime, or any other issue of concern to you). Do these things:

- ▶ Describe the issue and some specific problems.
- ▶ Ask what steps the city is taking to resolve the problems. Take notes.
- ▶ Give your suggestions for dealing with the problems.
- ▶ Ask your representative how you can help.

In the News: Get the Facts!

Collect at least three articles about how people have improved their communities by working with government to create change. Look for factors that contributed to their success. Make and fill out a chart like the one below.

Source and Date	Community Improvement	Success Factors
The Reporter November 10	**Incidents of crime and violence by young people reduced by over 50 percent**	**Leaders from neighborhood work together to solve own problems**
	Two-year effort to create activities that appeal to young people	**Government provides support and encouragement**
	College tuition provided for youth who stay out of trouble	

When you complete the chart, identify common success factors. Could these factors be used to solve other community problems? Why or why not?

Creative Works: React!

More than 200 people own units in the Aspen Condominiums and belong to the homeowners' association. Three times a year, owners meet to make rules and discuss housing issues, but few owners attend and show interest.

Create a poster that will convince condominium owners to attend meetings. It should show that owners have the power to make decisions about their condominiums, just as U.S. citizens have the power to make decisions about their government.

Inside Information

The Pledge of Allegiance

Many events begin with people joining together to repeat the pledge of allegiance to the flag of the United States. It is one way people show their loyalty to the country.

As you say the pledge of allegiance, stand and face the flag. Place your right hand over your heart, and repeat these words.

I pledge allegiance to the flag of the United States of America, and to the Republic for which it stands, one Nation, under God, indivisible, with liberty and justice for all.

Now, in your own words, write what the pledge means.

_____

_____

_____

Do other countries have a similar loyalty pledge?

Now check your progress on Unit 12, *Fall from Grace, Part 1.* Turn to page 150.

13 Fall from Grace, Part 2

In the United States, citizens elect people to represent them in government.

In this episode, tenants believe a city council member has abused their trust.

What can people do when elected officials misuse their power?

Preview the Story

Look at the pictures. Think about these questions. Share your ideas with someone.

What do you see?

What are these people thinking? What are they feeling?

What do you think will happen?

Preview Turning Points

In the United States, most elected officials are dedicated to their jobs and the people they represent. But what happens when people in authority misuse their position and power?

Think about the ideas above as you look at the pictures.

Think about these questions. Share your answers with someone.

Where do elected officials get their power?

What do you expect from responsible public officials?

How can public officials misuse power?

Remember the Story

🔔 **Read what people said. Look at the pictures. Complete the chart.**

Carla Castillo

Mayor Reilly

Amanda Hathaway

Roberto Sanchez

Ernesto

Crowd of people

What People Said	Who Said It	To Whom
1. "I had no idea this real estate partnership might be involved in something illegal."	Amanda Hathaway	Carla Castillo
2. "Try that, and they think you are a troublemaker. Next thing, your family is out on the street."		
3. "I think you need to step down."		
4. "The city is my life. I've done some things I'm really proud of."		
5. "Please sign the petitions and join me in recalling Councilwoman Hathaway."		
6. "I always accepted that it was the price we had to pay to be in this country, that things would never change. But maybe things can be different."		

🔔 🔔 **Put the paragraphs in order. Number them 1 to 5.**

_____ a. From a window in her office at City Hall, Hathaway sees a protest rally. Petitioners are gathering signatures. <u>Demonstrators</u> are carrying anti-Hathaway signs. Hathaway takes an award down from the wall and begins packing her things.

_____ b. The tenants take action. Ernesto speaks to groups, urging them to sign the <u>petition</u> to <u>recall</u> Councilwoman Hathaway. Roberto and others circulate recall petitions in a shopping center. Teresa attends a meeting of Hathaway <u>supporters</u>.

___1___ c. *Metro 5 News* reporter Carla Castillo has alleged that Councilwoman Amanda Hathaway is an owner of the Evergreen Apartments, which don't meet safety standards. The story begins to interfere with the work of the City Council, but Hathaway refuses to <u>resign</u>.

_____ d. Many of the tenants aren't citizens. They can't sign a recall petition. But they can get signatures of people who are <u>registered</u> to vote. Everyone supports the recall plan except Teresa—whose son attends a school that Hathaway worked to build.

_____ e. Tenants at the Evergreen Apartments meet. One suggests they vote Hathaway out of office. Another doesn't want to wait for the next election. Ernesto, who is <u>chairing</u> the meeting, suggests a special election to get her out of office.

Write the underlined words in the paragraphs next to their definitions below.

1. people who protest or support something in public

   demonstrators

2. act of presiding over or leading a meeting

   _____

3. formal written request to an official person or organization

   _____

4. to remove a public official from office by popular vote during his or her term

   _____

5. people in favor of a person, group, or plan

   _____

6. officially able to vote

   _____

7. to give up one's office or position

   _____

🔔 🔔 🔔 **Imagine that Diane Clayton talks with Roberto Sanchez after he finds out who owns the Evergreen Apartments. Role-play with someone. Your partner is Diane. You are Roberto.**

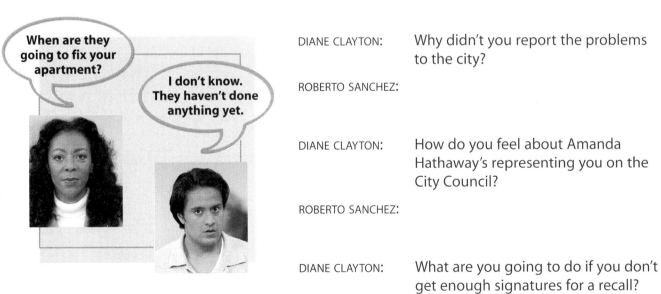

When are they going to fix your apartment?

I don't know. They haven't done anything yet.

DIANE CLAYTON: Why didn't you report the problems to the city?

ROBERTO SANCHEZ:

DIANE CLAYTON: How do you feel about Amanda Hathaway's representing you on the City Council?

ROBERTO SANCHEZ:

DIANE CLAYTON: What are you going to do if you don't get enough signatures for a recall?

ROBERTO SANCHEZ:

Remember Turning Points

Write *T (True)* or *F (False)* next to each statement.

___T___ 1. In the United States, many different people and institutions carry out the responsibilities of government.

_____ 2. Citizens can do very little when elected public officials misuse their positions and power.

_____ 3. If a federal official is charged with violating the law, Congress may impeach and remove that official from office.

_____ 4. Election to public office allows candidates to do what they want in office.

_____ 5. Election to public office is a contract of trust between voters and the people they choose to represent them.

What strategies can be used to remove these two representatives from office? Read the situation. Then make two lists using options from the box on the right. An option may be used in both lists or not used at all.

Two members of Congress, Representative A and Representative B, have abused the trust of the voters in their districts. Representative A has a poor voting record. He has missed voting on important bills and does not respond to calls or requests from people in his district. Representative B has taken money in exchange for her vote and has accepted gifts and trips from major special-interest groups.

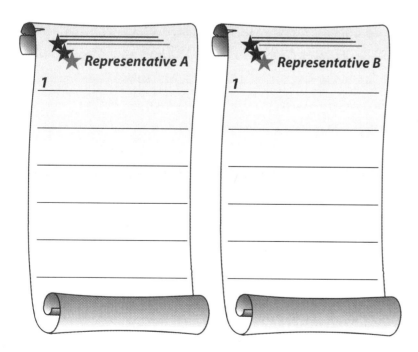

Representative A

1 _____
_____
_____
_____
_____
_____

Representative B

1 _____
_____
_____
_____
_____
_____

Options

1. Representative recalled by voters.

2. Colleagues convince member to resign.

3. President signs executive order to remove person from office.

4. Supreme Court rules that person cannot hold office.

5. Congress impeaches, tries, and removes from office.

6. People in district do not vote for person in next election.

When a member of Congress misuses power, various people and groups can take action to stop the abuse. Read the list of persons and groups. Write the action each person or group can take.

Who	Action
1. public official	*convince the elected official to resign from office*
2. citizen	
3. Congress	
4. reporter	

Making Connections

Read the quote below. Think about the questions. Share your answers with someone.

> Election to public office is a contract of trust between voters and the people they choose to represent them.

 In this episode, who violates the voters' trust?

 How do the mayor and the City Council respond to the elected official who violates the contract of trust?

 What do people do about the violation? What else can they do?

How can U.S. citizens exercise political power?

The political system of the United States is designed to give people the chance to exercise authority over government and to participate in the political process.

▶ The citizens of the United States vote for the people who will represent them at all levels of government, from president of the country to members of the local school board. Sometimes citizens also vote on issues, such as building schools or increasing local taxes.

▶ Some citizens take an active role in government by running for **public office**. Others volunteer to serve on boards or commissions. When people accept an elected or appointed position, they also accept certain responsibilities. They must study the issues, and they must make decisions that they think are best for the community that they serve.

▶ Some citizens do not run for office, but they work for the election of a candidate or a cause that they believe in. They volunteer to help with campaigns. They also join special-interest groups that share their ideas.

You can make a difference if you learn about government and how it works, study the issues, and voice your opinions.

What are the rights and responsibilities of people in the United States?

Although many of the responsibilities of people in the United States are not required by law, they are essential for the **common good**—for the well-being of neighborhoods, towns, states, and the country. Each person can help to create a better way of life.

Lawful permanent residents in the United States have many of the same rights as citizens. They have the right to due process—the right to be protected by this country's laws. But they don't have the right to vote and the right to hold public office.

Citizens and noncitizens alike must do these things:

▶ obey the country's laws

▶ pay income, sales, and property taxes

▶ send their children to school (Age requirements vary from state to state, but usually children must attend school from age five or six to at least age sixteen.)

▶ register for the draft at age 18 if they are male (This means that they can be called to serve in the armed forces in a national emergency.)

In addition, citizens can be called to serve on a jury or as witnesses in court. Lawful residents cannot serve on a jury, but they may be called as witnesses in court.

What is the difference between a democracy and a dictatorship?

The role of a citizen in a constitutional **democracy** is different from the role of a citizen living under a **dictatorship**. In a dictatorship, citizens are expected to be obedient and loyal no matter what the government does. But in a democracy, citizens can freely ask questions and take part in the political community.

Use information in the reading on pages 70 and 71 to complete the sentences. Underline or highlight the sentence in the reading that supports your answer. Then write the sentence in the space below the choices.

1. In the United States, citizens decide to build a new school by
   a. voting for a bond issue.
   b. calling the president and members of the school board.
   c. holding a public debate.

Sometimes citizens also vote on issues, such as building schools or increasing local taxes.

2. All U.S. citizens should
   a. run for political office.
   b. be obedient and follow orders.
   c. contribute to the common good.

3. Lawful permanent residents in the United States do not have the right to
   a. hold public office.
   b. protest in public.
   c. purchase property.

4. The citizens of a constitutional democracy
   a. try not to question their government.
   b. have the right to participate in political activities.
   c. give their leaders absolute power.

Complete the sentences. Use your own words.

1. Three ways that people can participate in the U.S. political system are _____

2. Three things that both citizens and lawful permanent residents are required to do in the United States are _____

Think about the questions. Share your answers with someone.

1. How can citizens exercise their power?

2. How do you contribute to your community?

Pick Your Project

Do one or more of the following activities. Share your work with someone.

Community Matters: Interact!

Interview two people about a current or recent mayor, governor, or president. Ask these questions. Ask for reasons or examples. Take notes.

- ▶ Is this person honest?
- ▶ Is this person good with people?
- ▶ Is this person respected?

- ▶ Is this person good at getting things done?
- ▶ What will you remember this person for?

In the News: Get the Facts!

Read the Letters to the Editor column for several days. Collect letters from at least four different people about one issue of concern to people in your city. See if you can also find articles on the same issue that report the positions of special-interest groups, unions, and professional organizations. Make a chart like the one below.

Source and Date	Issue	Position
Letter from Luis Alvarez **Press-Telegram** **June 5**	**Building new $6 million sports complex**	**The city should not take on this debt with so many greater needs—high unemployment, poor schools, not enough low-cost housing for senior citizens.**
Chamber of Commerce **Morning Globe** **June 3**		**The city needs the complex to attract major professional teams. Additional tax revenue should pay off debt in 15 years. Jobs will be created; everyone will benefit.**

Which arguments appear to be based on emotion rather than logic, on opinions rather than facts? What kind of arguments do you think will be most effective in influencing government action? Which side do you favor, and why?

Creative Works: React!

Write a campaign speech for an office you or a friend would like to run for. The office can be at the local, state, or national level. Address these points in your speech.

- ▶ problems in your community
- ▶ how you would improve your community
- ▶ why people should vote for you

Fall from Grace, Part 2

Inside Information

All nations have patriotic songs that express people's love for their country. Some are old folk songs. Many were written at the time of war or revolution. This is the story of the *Star-Spangled Banner*, adopted by Congress as the national anthem in 1931.

1. In 1814, British armed forces set fire to the Capitol and other buildings in Washington, D.C.

2. The attackers took a prisoner with them when they returned to their ships, which were anchored nearby.

3. Frances Scott Key, a young lawyer, asked President Madison's permission to rescue the prisoner, and Madison agreed.

4. Key found the ships preparing to attack the city of Baltimore near the place where the Potomac River meets the Atlantic Ocean.

7. But at night they could see only bombshells "bursting in air." They anxiously paced on the deck of the ship, waiting for the dawn. When the sun rose, Key saw the U.S. flag still waving in

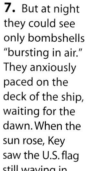

5. The British agreed to release the prisoner to Key after the battle.

6. During the battle the next day, Key and the prisoner saw the U.S. flag flying over the fort that guarded the city.

the breeze above the fort. Inspired, he wrote the words to the national anthem on the back of an envelope.

> *O say, can you see by the dawn's early light,*
> *What so proudly we hailed at the twilight's last gleaming?*
> *Whose broad stripes and bright stars, through the perilous fight,*
> *O'er the ramparts we watched, were so gallantly streaming.*
> *And the rockets' red glare, the bombs bursting in air,*
> *Gave proof through the night that our flag was still there.*
> *O say, does that star-spangled banner yet wave*
> *O'er the land of the free, and the home of the brave?*

w check your progress on Unit 13, *Fall from Grace, Part 2.* **Turn to page 152.**

73

non Ground

14 Skin Deep

Many immigrants come to the United States to find work and a better life.

In this episode, an immigrant business owner has a conflict with another business owner.

What can business owners do to protect their economic rights?

Preview the Story

Look at the pictures. Think about these questions. Share your ideas with someone.

What do you see?

What are these people thinking? What are they feeling?

What do you think will happen?

Preview Turning Points

Many people have immigrated to the United States to find work and achieve a better life.

Think about the ideas above as you look at the pictures.

Think about these questions. Share your answers with someone.

- What kind of work or life have immigrants found in the United States?
- Why did you or someone you know come to the United States?
- How have your thoughts about opportunities in the United States changed through the years?

Remember the Story

Read what people said. Look at the pictures. Complete the chart.

Grace Ardmore

Carla Castillo

City Council

Sam Hasharian

Jess Holcomb

Police officer

Derek Powell

Walter Prescott
Councilman

Mayor Reilly

Nate Thompson
Councilman

What People Said	Who Said It	To Whom
1. "I don't know what you saw, or what you think you saw, but there is nothing illegal going on outside your store."	Police officer	Grace Ardmore
2. "This would be a renovation project from the ground up. The mayor thinks it could make a real difference."		
3. "I have broken no laws. A neighbor was angry at my customers. Now it looks like the entire … city is against me."		
4. "You can inform Prescott that this office is not in the business of harassing innocent store owners."		
5. "My line of work, as you call it, is what I must do to support my family."		
6. "All I want is for this city to make an investment in the people who live and work in my district."		

Put the paragraphs in order. Number them 1 to 5.

_____ a. Mayor Reilly learns from a *Metro 5 News* broadcast that the city has closed the tattoo parlor while inspectors check for <u>health and safety violations</u>. Powell tells him that closing the tattoo parlor was Prescott's price for supporting the Third Street <u>renovation</u>. The mayor says the city should not harass innocent store owners.

___1___ b. Grace Ardmore owns an elegant dress shop. Customers from the tattoo parlor next door play loud music as they wait on the sidewalk. Grace is losing business. She wants the police to arrest the tattoo shop customers for <u>disturbing the peace</u>. The police tell her the people are not doing anything illegal.

_____ c. The tattoo parlor is in the district of City Councilman Walter Prescott. Derek Powell, the mayor's assistant, asks Prescott to support a proposal to renovate Third Street. Prescott wants something in exchange for his support. He wants the tattoo parlor out of his district. He wants his <u>constituents</u> to be happy.

_____ d. The Mayor doesn't want a lawsuit, but he needs to have the Third Street project approved. He tells Powell to make the deal with Prescott, but to be sure it includes money to relocate Hasharian.

_____ e. Nate Thompson introduced the plan for the renovation of Third Street many months ago. Now people from the district are threatening to file a <u>class-action lawsuit</u> because the city has done nothing with the plan.

Write the underlined words in the paragraphs next to their definitions below.

1. people living in an elected official's district   _____

2. improvement made by repairing or remodeling a building or neighborhood   _____

3. problem that a group of people take to a court of law   _____

4. annoying, interfering with, or disrupting the activities of others   _____

5. failures to keep an area clean and safe   ___*health and safety violations*___

🔔 🔔 🔔 **Imagine that Danny Hasharian talks to his father, Sam Hasharian. Role-play with someone. Your partner is Danny. You are Sam.**

> Dad, why do you have to own a tattoo parlor?

> I have to make money to support our family.

DANNY: Some kids say you are ruining the neighborhood. What should I tell them?

SAM:

DANNY: Can't you move your business to another street?

SAM:

DANNY: I'm tired of this. Why did we come to this country?

SAM:

Remember Turning Points

Write *T (True)* or *F (False)* next to each statement.

__F__ 1. In the early days of the colonies, both land and labor were abundant.

_____ 2. Many colonists paid the cost of ship passage for young men who agreed to work for them for four to seven years without pay.

_____ 3. Most immigrants left their home countries because of political or religious persecution, crop failure, famine, or loss of jobs.

_____ 4. Immigrants contributed enormously to the changing American scene, doubling the population of the country in just a few years.

_____ 5. But after the first few decades, the desire to immigrate to the United States decreased as countries around the world achieved economic and political stability.

Read the phrases on the right. Look at the chart. Write each phrase in one of the columns in the chart. Check each phrase after you use it.

Reasons for Leaving Home Country	
Economic Reasons	*Other Reasons*
	1. political persecution

1. political persecution ✔

2. crop failure

3. famine

4. loss of jobs

5. religious persecution

6. revolution

7. war

Fill in the chart. List at least three opportunities for immigrants in their new country. Then list at least three contributions of immigrants who took advantage of the opportunities.

Opportunities	Immigrant Contributions
1. *abundance of land*	*farmed the land*
2.	
3.	
4.	

Making Connections

Read the statement below. Think about the questions. Share your answers with someone.

> Common reasons that people immigrate to the United States are to find work and achieve a better life.

In this story, what kind of work does Sam Hasharian do? Why?

How do the neighbors feel about his business? Why? What did each of these people do to try to change things?

- ▶ the owner of the business next door
- ▶ the councilman from the district
- ▶ people from the Department of Health and Safety
- ▶ the people from the neighborhood

What happens in the end? What else might have happened?

What economic powers does the Constitution give Congress?

The **Framers** of the Constitution—the people who wrote the Constitution—wanted to be sure that the economy of the new nation could grow and be strong. As they wrote the Constitution, they gave Congress these powers:

- ▶ to collect taxes
- ▶ to borrow money
- ▶ to regulate business—between states and also with other nations
- ▶ to coin or issue money and regulate its value

The states did not have the right to coin money or enter into **treaties** with foreign nations.

What economic rights do people have in the United States?

The only reference to the economic rights of the individual in the Constitution is found in the Fifth and the Fourteenth Amendments. These amendments state that no person shall lose life, liberty, or property without due process of law. This means that no one can take away what someone else has worked for and owns without a reason based on law.

People in the United States have several kinds of economic rights. Most of these rights are the result of legislative and court decisions.

People have the right to buy, own, and sell property.

People have the right to choose the kind of work they do, and they have the right to change jobs.

People have the right to join labor unions and professional associations.

People have the right to establish and operate a business.

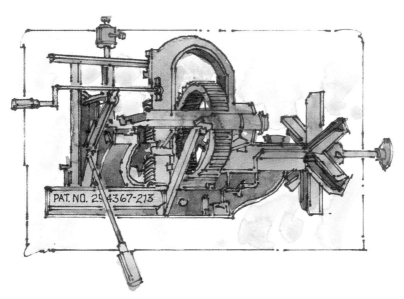

Someone who invents a new product or process has the right to protect that idea with a **copyright** or **patent**.

Use information in the reading on pages 82 and 83 to complete the sentences. Underline or highlight the sentence in the reading that supports your answer. Then write the sentence in the space below the choices.

1. The men who wrote the Constitution wanted to help the country's economy
   a. stay the same as it was.
   b. grow and become stronger.
   c. become the strongest in the world.

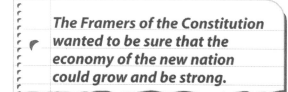

The Framers of the Constitution wanted to be sure that the economy of the new nation could grow and be strong.

2. The Constitution does not allow states
   a. to make coins or issue money.
   b. to elect legislators.
   c. to attract new businesses.

3. A patent is a legal document that protects
   a. new ideas or products.
   b. professional associations.
   c. the power to coin money.

4. U.S. workers
   a. must join a labor union.
   b. cannot join a labor union.
   c. can join a labor union.

Complete the sentences. Use your own words.

1. The Constitution gives Congress the economic power to _____

   _____

2. Two economic rights of U.S. citizens are _____

   _____

Think about the questions. Share your answers with someone.

1. Why does the Constitution give the power to coin money to Congress but not to the states?

2. Tell at least one way that individuals' economic rights help the economy of the country.

Pick Your Project

Do one or more of the following activities. Share your work with someone.

Community Matters: Interact!

Interview two people who own small businesses, such as a bookkeeping service, laundromat, lawn care service, auto repair shop, and so on. Ask these questions and take notes.

▶ When did you start this business?
▶ Why did you start it?
▶ Did you have any problems in the beginning?
▶ What advice do you have for other people who want to start a new small business?

In the News: Get the Facts!

Collect at least three newspaper and magazine articles about different economic actions taken by the federal government. Relate each action to the economic power of Congress to collect taxes, to borrow money, to regulate business, or to regulate the value of money.

Make and fill out a chart like the one below to identify the action and the congressional power it represents.

Source of Information	Action and Congressional Power
New Voices **July 1, 1998**	● ACTION: **interest rates lowered by Federal Reserve chairman** ● CONGRESSIONAL POWER: **to regulate the value of money**

When you complete the chart, look at the different types of economic activities in which the government is involved. What conclusions can you make about the influence government has on the economy?

Creative Works: React!

Create a simple guide for young people who would like to start a small business. The business might provide a service such as babysitting or lawn care, or it might involve a product they create and sell.

The guide should include such topics as these:

▶ the need for the service or product
▶ the competition
▶ government regulations that apply
▶ the importance of quality work

▶ expenses involved in providing the service or product
▶ determining what to charge
▶ low-cost advertising

Inside Information

Read the descriptions of five immigrants who found the same kind of jobs in the United States that they had in their own countries. Look at the map and the map key at the left. Where do you think those jobs would be located?

Write the letter for each immigrant on a region of the map where that person could find a job. If you don't know enough about some regions of the country, ask someone.

a. Pablo was a farmer who grew wheat and corn.

b. Tuan was a mining engineer.

c. Sophia was a ski instructor.

d. Jacques was a lobster fisherman

e. Sven was a lumberman.

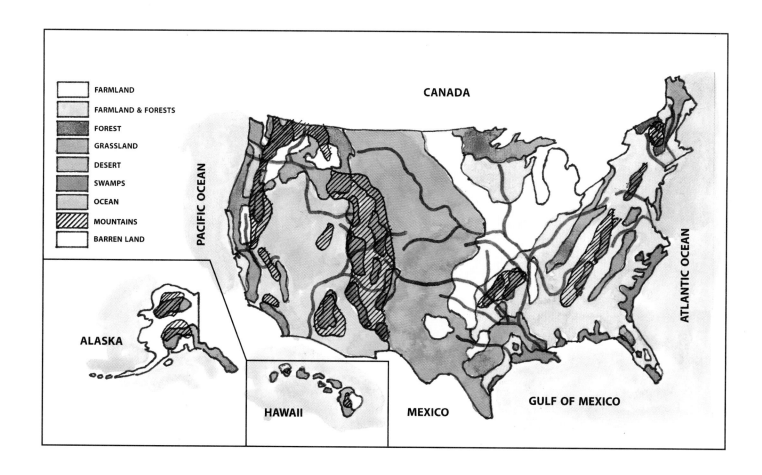

Now check your progress on Unit 14, *Skin Deep*. Turn to page 154.

15 Hidden Agenda

The Constitution of the United States supports fair treatment and equal opportunities for all people.

In this episode, some maintenance workers and a television news anchor are treated unfairly.

What can people do to protest in these situations?

Preview the Story

Look at the pictures from each story. Think about these questions. Share your ideas with someone.

What do you see?

What are these people thinking? What are they feeling?

What do you think will happen?

The Workers' Story

Katherine's Story

Preview Turning Points

Sometimes people don't get fair treatment or equal opportunities. Laws can protect against unfair treatment and discrimination.

Think about the ideas above as you look at the pictures.

Think about these questions. Share your answers with someone.

Who wants change and why?

Have you ever been treated unfairly? Have you seen other people treated unfairly? Why do you think it happened?

What could you have done? What could other people have done?

Remember the Story

The Workers' Story

Read what people said. Look at the pictures. Complete the chart.

Carla Castillo

Jess Holcomb
City Attorney

Derek Powell

Mayor Reilly

Mr. Lee

Older worker

Supervisor

TV audience

Worker

What People Said	Who Said It	To Whom
1. "Fever very high. Ask if …can go home, but they say no."	*Worker*	*Carla Castillo*
2. "Stories about workplace abuse seem almost commonplace these days."		
3. "We don't want the city employing a vendor who's breaking labor laws."		
4. "My workers are like my own family. I would never mistreat them."		
5. "What do you think you're doing? You don't have time to relax. Get back to work."		

Put the paragraphs in order. Number them 1 to 5.

_____ a. But when the city attorney meets with Mr. Lee, the owner of Metropolitan Cleaning, Mr. Lee denies the charges saying, "With over 200 employees, why would only one person speak out? Maybe a <u>competitor</u> is trying to make me look bad."

_____ b. After the news report, Mayor Reilly and Derek Powell ask City Attorney Holcomb about the cleaning company. The owner has been in business for years, had good <u>references</u>, and offered the best price. They agree to investigate the charges.

_____ c. Carla finds a reason to go to City Hall at night. She sees workers cleaning and a supervisor forcing an older man who is ill to work without a rest. Carla thinks this might be a case of <u>workplace abuse</u>.

___1___ d. Carla interviews a worker on *Metro 5 News*. He works for Metropolitan Cleaning, a company that has the <u>contract</u> to clean city buildings. He says that the company didn't let him go home when he was sick and doesn't pay for <u>overtime</u> work.

_____ e. The city attorney confronts Mr. Lee again, this time with evidence of <u>labor law</u> violations. Several workers are ready to tell their story. The Department of Employment and Fair Housing files a lawsuit for the workers against Metropolitan Cleaning.

Write the underlined words in the paragraphs next to their definitions below.

1. unfair treatment of employees by someone in authority

   _____

2. extra hours of work beyond the standard day or week

   _____

3. company or person that tries to be more successful than others that offer the same products or services

   _____ *competitor* _____

4. legal agreement between two or more people or companies

   _____

5. related to rules made by a government about work

   _____

6. recommendations from people who used services of a company or person

   _____

🔔 🔔 🔔   **Imagine that Carla interviews Mr. Lee. Role-play with someone. Your partner is Carla. You are Mr. Lee.**

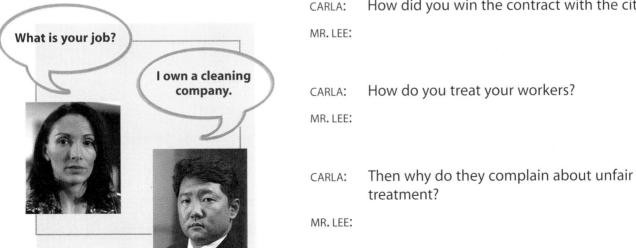

CARLA: How did you win the contract with the city?

MR. LEE:

CARLA: How do you treat your workers?

MR. LEE:

CARLA: Then why do they complain about unfair treatment?

MR. LEE:

Remember the Story

Katherine's Story

🔔 **Read what people said. Look at the pictures. Complete the chart.**

Carla Castillo

John Sweeney
News Anchor

Katherine Morrison
News Anchor

TV audience

Tom Hendricks
Station Manager

Steve Richards
News Producer

What People Said	Who Said It	To Whom
1. "The owners of the station want to let you go."	*Tom Hendricks*	*Katherine Morrison*
2. "I've put 15 years of my life into this job, and you want to tell me it's business!"		
3. "Joining me tonight is Nadine Taylor, the newest addition to our *Six O'Clock News* family."		
4. "I want you to look me straight in the eye and tell me why I was fired."		
5. "Why are we the only station in town not covering the Katherine Morrison story?"		

🔔 🔔 **Put the paragraphs in order. Number them 1 to 6.**

_____ a. Katherine sees John Sweeney, her former co-anchor, at the park. He tells her that she has a lot of public support. He suggests that she fight the television station and offers to testify for her.

_____ b. The news producer tells Carla that "ratings go to news shows with anchors that people like to look at." Carla says, "In other words, Katherine was too old." To Carla, this is <u>discrimination</u>.

_____ c. Carla wonders why *Metro 5 News* is not reporting on Katherine's lawsuit. She says that a news anchor suing a television station over a possible <u>civil rights</u> violation *is* important news.

_____ d. Carla surprises her co-workers at *Metro 5 News* when she reports about Morrison's lawsuit. The lawsuit <u>alleges</u> that the station <u>violated</u> Morrison's civil rights.

__*1*__ e. A TV station <u>fires</u> news anchor Katherine Morrison. Katherine discovers that the station has replaced her with a much younger woman. She suspects that she has been fired because she has a "few too many wrinkles." This action violates "every <u>ethical</u> code in the book."

Write the underlined words in the paragraphs next to their definitions below.

1. acted against the law

2. relating to principles of right and wrong

3. related to privileges that people have as members of society

4. states without proof or before getting proof

5. unfair treatment, especially because of race, religion, age, or sex

   discrimination

6. ends a person's employment

🔔 🔔 🔔 **Imagine that Carla interviews Katherine Morrison. Role-play with someone. Your partner is Carla. You are Katherine.**

What was your job?

I was a TV news anchor.

CARLA: Why do you think they fired you?

KATHERINE:

CARLA: What will you do about it?

KATHERINE:

CARLA: Will this help or hurt your chances of getting another anchor position?

KATHERINE:

Remember Turning Points

🔔 **Match each situation with a category. Write a letter on the line.**

     a. civil rights violation   b. unfair labor practice   c. the right to protest

b 1. young children working in a factory

_____ 2. women arguing for the right to vote

_____ 3. unhealthy working conditions in a coal mine

_____ 4. bus stop for "whites only"

_____ 5. civil rights march

_____ 6. confinement of Japanese families during World War II

_____ 7. farm workers urging people not to buy grapes and lettuce

🔔 🔔 **Review the words in the box. The flow chart below them shows steps leading to change. Write the words in the flow chart. Put a check by each word or phrase after you use it.**

change	civil rights violations	discrimination ✔
protests ✔	unfair labor practices	

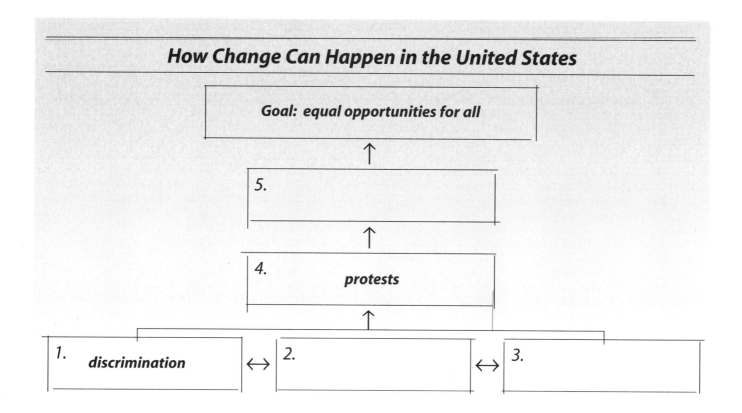

How Change Can Happen in the United States

Goal: equal opportunities for all

↑

5.

↑

4. *protests*

↑

1. *discrimination* ↔ 2. ↔ 3.

Read the words on the left. Give one example for each.

Shared Value	Example
1. equal opportunities	*Two people receive the same pay for the same job.*
2. civil rights	
3. fair labor practices	
4. right to public protest	
5. peaceful change	

Making Connections

Read the quotes below. Think about the questions. Share your answers with someone.

Unfair Labor Practices

> Even in a country that tries to provide equal opportunities for all people, reality doesn't always match the ideal.

In this story, who was the victim of unfair labor practices?

What was the unfair labor practice? Why was it unfair?

What was done about it? What else might have been done?

Discrimination

> Examples of discrimination, of civil rights violations, darken the pages of American history.

In this story, who experienced discrimination?

What was the discrimination? Why was this unfair?

What was done about it? What else could have been done?

> The Constitution is "intended to endure for ages to come, and consequently, to be adapted to the various crises of human affairs."
> —Chief Justice John Marshall, 1787

Why is the U.S. Constitution such a lasting document?

The Constitution of the United States has lasted for more than two hundred years, longer than the constitution of any other country. Why has the Constitution lasted so long? It allows for change—through amendments that are agreed to by most of the states, through **court rulings**, and through the **legislative process**.

This ability to change with the times has helped to create greater equality of opportunity for all U.S. citizens. The Fourteenth Amendment to the Constitution promised **equal protection under the law.** In recent years, court rulings and **legislation** have further defined the words "equal protection."

How have court rulings helped to increase equal opportunities?

Linda Brown's Story

Linda Brown lived only five blocks from a school for white children. By law, she had to attend a school for black children twenty-one blocks away. Linda's parents, and the parents of other black students, sued for the right to send their children to the neighborhood school.

Eventually, the case reached the Supreme Court. The attorney for the black families argued that separate schools harm both black and white children. The Supreme Court agreed. In 1954, it ruled that separate schools violate the principle of equal protection found in the Fourteenth Amendment.

Ida Phillips' Story

Ida Phillips applied for a position with the Martin Marietta Corporation in 1966. When she was interviewed, they asked her if she had children. The company felt that young children take up a lot of a woman's time and energy. Because Ida Phillips had two pre-school children, she was not hired.

Phillips decided to sue the company. Her lawyers argued that she was not treated equally. Men who were applying for a job were not asked about their children. In fact, they were hired whether or not they had children.

After studying the case, the court ruled in favor of Phillips. Martin Marietta had not proved that children get in the way of a mother's job performance. There should not be one hiring policy for women and another for men.

What contributions has legislation made?

Legislation is often the result of **public pressure** and court decisions. In recent years, **Congress** has expanded the equal protection clause of the Fourteenth Amendment to prevent discrimination on the basis of age, sex, and ethnic background, as well as race.

Congress has also passed federal laws to protect the rights of workers against unfair labor practices and acts of abuse. Here are a few examples of the laws that have been passed.

▶ **Child Labor Laws— Fair Labor Standards Act, 1938**

Limits when, where, and how many hours children under sixteen can work.

▶ **Equal Pay Act—Fair Labor Standards Act, 1963**

Prohibits discrimination in pay on the basis of sex.

▶ **Civil Rights Act of 1964**

Protects the rights of individuals to fair treatment by private persons, groups, organizations, businesses, and government.

▶ **Age Discrimination in Employment Act, 1967**

Protects workers from age forty to age seventy from unfair employment decisions based on age.

▶ **Equal Employment Opportunity Act—1972 amendment to Title VII, Civil Rights Act of 1964**

Protects employees and applicants from discrimination related to compensation (pay), terms, conditions, or privileges of employment because of a person's race, color, religion, sex, or national origin.

Use information in the reading on pages 96 and 97 to complete the sentences. Underline or highlight the sentence in the reading that supports your answer. Then write the sentence in the space below the choices.

1. The Constitution allows for change through
   a. war and revolution.
   b. court decisions and laws.
   c. schools and corporations.

   It allows for change—through amendments that are agreed to by most of the states, through court rulings, and through the legislative process.

2. Before 1954, Linda Brown had to
   a. go to school with white children.
   b. go to school with black children.
   c. stay at home for school.

3. Ida Phillips did not get the job because she
   a. was too old.
   b. could not type.
   c. had small children.

4. The legislation that prohibits discrimination in wages on the basis of sex is the
   a. Equal Pay Act.
   b. Equal Employment Opportunity Act.
   c. Civil Rights Act.

Complete the sentences. Use your own words.

1. The Supreme Court ruled that Linda Brown suffered discrimination because

   _____

2. Congress passed laws on civil rights and labor practices because of _____

   _____

Think about the questions. Share your answers with someone.

1. How did the Supreme Court cases involving Linda Brown and Ida Phillips affect the lives of people in the United States?

2. Which law listed on page 97 affects you most? How?

Pick Your Project

Do one or more of the following activities. Share your work with someone.

Community Matters: Interact!

Contact your local office of the Equal Employment Opportunity Commission or the Department of Labor. Ask for information about fair labor practices in your state. Ask questions like the ones below and take notes.

▶ How can I find out about fair labor practices?
▶ Is it legal for some jobs to have age limitations?
▶ Is it legal for an employer to ask on a job application if an applicant has children?
▶ What can I do if I think I'm being treated unfairly on my job?

In the News: Get the Facts!

Collect at least three newspaper articles on civil rights violations or unfair labor practices. Read the articles. As you read, highlight the main idea in each article. Then make a chart like the one below.

Source and Date	Main Idea
National Reporter *March 7*	**Women and minorities will get equal opportunities under Disadvantaged Business Enterprise Program.**

When you complete the chart, study the main ideas and think about all the articles. Are there similarities in types of violations, places they occur, results, and so on? What conclusions can you make about civil rights and labor practices in the U.S. today?

Creative Works: React!

Use your imagination and the information in this unit to draw a comic strip illustrating Katherine's story or the workers' story. Before you begin, look at some comic strips to see how they tell the story. Use at least five frames, or panels, to show characters and action. Use speech bubbles to show what the characters say. The way you draw each character should show what you think of that person.

Inside Information

Holiday Traditions

Holiday traditions create a common bond among people. In the United States, holidays often celebrate important events in the history of the nation. For example, Thanksgiving is a special day observed each November. It's a tradition to roast a turkey and prepare a large meal to share with family members

and friends. The Pilgrims and the Indians celebrated the first Thanksgiving in the 1600s. The Pilgrims, newly settled in the "New World," wanted to give thanks for the harvest and the help the Indians had given them.

July 4th celebrates the signing of the Declaration of Independence in 1776. Cities and towns across the country have parades and fireworks in honor of the day. It's a tradition to fly a flag from houses on July 4th. The colors red, white, and blue can be seen everywhere! Because it is a holiday from work for many people and the weather is warm, families often celebrate the day with a picnic.

Write about other U.S. holidays in the chart below. If you don't know about some of the holidays, ask someone.

Holiday and Date	Why this day is celebrated	Tradition
MARTIN LUTHER KING DAY third Monday in January	**To honor contributions of civil rights leader Dr. Martin Luther King, Jr.**	**speeches and parades**
PRESIDENT'S DAY third Monday in February		
MEMORIAL DAY fourth Monday in May		
LABOR DAY first Monday in September		
VETERANS DAY November 11		

Now check your progress on Unit 15, *Hidden Agenda*. Turn to page 156.

PREAMBLE

We the People of the United States, in Order to form a more perfect Union, establish Justice, insure domestic Tranquility, provide for the common defence, promote the general Welfare, and secure the Blessings of Liberty to ourselves and our Posterity, do ordain and establish this Constitution for the United States of America.

ARTICLE I

Section I

All legislative Powers herein granted shall be vested in a Congress of the United States, which shall consist of a Senate and House of Representatives.

Section 2

1. The House of Representatives shall be composed of Members chosen every second Year by the People of the several States, and the Electors in each State shall have the Qualifications requisite for Electors of the most numerous Branch of the State Legislature.

2. No Person shall be a Representative who shall not have attained to the Age of twenty five Years, and been seven Years a Citizen of the United States, and who shall not, when elected, be an Inhabitant of that State in which he shall be chosen.

3. [Representatives and direct Taxes shall be apportioned among the several States which may be included within this Union, according to their respective Numbers, which shall be determined by adding to the whole Number of free Persons, including those bound to Service for a Term of Years, and excluding Indians not taxed, three fifths of all other Persons.][1] The actual Enumeration shall be made within three Years after the first Meeting of the Congress of the United States, and within every subsequent Term of ten Years, in such Manner as they shall by Law direct. The number of Representatives shall not exceed one for every thirty Thousand, but each State shall have at Least one Representative; and until such enumeration shall be made, the State of New Hampshire shall be entitled to choose three, Massachusetts eight, Rhode-Island and Providence Plantations one, Connecticut five, New York six, New Jersey four, Pennsylvania eight, Delaware one, Maryland six, Virginia ten, North Carolina five, South Carolina five, and Georgia three.

4. When vacancies happen in the Representation from any State, the Executive Authority thereof shall issue Writs of Election to fill such Vacancies.

5. The House of Representatives shall choose their Speaker and other Officers; and shall have the sole Power of Impeachment.

---

[1] (Throughout the Constitution, passages enclosed in brackets and marked with footnote numbers have been changed by amendment, as indicated.) Changed by Section 2 of the Fourteenth Amendment.

Section 3

1. The Senate of the United States shall be composed of two Senators from each State, [chosen by the Legislature thereof,]² for six Years; and each Senator shall have one Vote.

2. Immediately after they shall be assembled in consequence of the first Election, they shall be divided as equally as may be into three Classes. The Seats of the Senators of the first Class shall be vacated at the Expiration of the second Year, of the second Class at the Expiration of the fourth Year, and of the third Class at the Expiration of the sixth Year, so that one third may be chosen every second Year; [and if Vacancies happen by Resignation, or otherwise, during the Recess of the Legislature of any State, the Executive thereof may make temporary Appointments until the next Meeting of the Legislature, which shall then fill such Vacancies.]³

3. No Person shall be a Senator who shall not have attained to the Age of thirty Years, and been nine Years a Citizen of the United States, and who shall not, when elected, be an inhabitant of that State for which he shall be chosen.

4. The Vice President of the United States shall be President of the Senate, but shall have no vote, unless they be equally divided.

5. The Senate shall choose their other Officers, and also a President pro tempore, in the Absence of the Vice President, or when he shall exercise the Office of President of the United States.

6. The Senate shall have the sole Power to try all Impeachments. When sitting for that Purpose, they shall be on Oath or Affirmation. When the President of the United States is tried, the Chief Justice shall preside; and no Person shall be convicted without the Concurrence of two thirds of the Members present.

7. Judgment in Cases of Impeachment shall not extend further than to removal from Office, and disqualification to hold and enjoy any Office of Honor, Trust or Profit under the United States; but the Party convicted shall nevertheless be liable and subject to Indictment, Trial, Judgment and Punishment, according to Law.

Section 4

1. The Times, Places and Manner of holding Elections for Senators and Representatives shall be prescribed in each State by the legislature thereof, but the Congress may at any time by Law make or alter such Regulations, except as to the Places of choosing Senators.

2. The Congress shall assemble at least once in every Year, and such Meeting shall be [on the first Monday in December,]⁴ unless they shall by Law appoint a different Day.

Section 5

1. Each House shall be the Judge of the Elections, Returns and Qualifications of its own Members, and a Majority of each shall constitute a Quorum to do Business; but a smaller Number may adjourn from day to day, and may be authorized to compel the Attendance of absent Members, in such Manner, and under such Penalties as each House may provide.

---

² Changed by the Seventeenth Amendment.
³ Changed by the Seventeenth Amendment.
⁴ Changed by Section 2 of the Twentieth Amendment.

2. Each House may determine the Rules of its Proceedings, punish its Members for disorderly Behavior, and, with the Concurrence of two thirds, expel a Member.

3. Each House shall keep a journal of its Proceedings, and from time to time publish the same, excepting such Parts as may in their Judgment require Secrecy; and the Yeas and Nays of the Members of either House on any question shall, at the Desire of one fifth of those Present, be entered on the Journal.

4. Neither House, during the Session of Congress, shall, without the Consent of the other, adjourn for more than three days, nor to any other Place than that in which the two Houses shall be sitting.

Section 6

1. The Senators and Representatives shall receive a Compensation for their Services, to be ascertained by Law, and paid out of the Treasury of the United States. They shall in all Cases, except Treason, Felony, and Breach of the Peace be privileged from Arrest during their Attendance at the Session of their respective Houses, and in going to and returning from the same; and for any Speech or Debate in either House, they shall not be questioned in any other Place.

2. No Senator or Representative shall, during the Time for which he was elected, be appointed to any civil Office under the Authority of the United States, which shall have been created, or the Emoluments whereof shall have been increased during such time; and no Person holding any Office under the United States, shall be a Member of either House during his continuance in Office.

Section 7

1. All Bills for raising Revenue shall originate in the House of Representatives; but the Senate may propose or concur with Amendments as on other Bills.

2. Every Bill which shall have passed the House of Representatives and the Senate, shall, before it becomes a Law, be presented to the President of the United States; if he approves he shall sign it, but if not he shall return it, with his Objections, to that House in which it shall have originated, who shall enter the Objections at large on their Journal, and proceed to Reconsider it. If after such reconsideration two thirds of that House shall agree to pass the Bill, it shall be sent, together with the Objections, to the other House, by which it shall likewise be reconsidered, and if approved by two thirds of that House, it shall become a Law. But in all such cases the votes of both Houses shall be determined by Yeas and Nays, and the Names of the Persons voting for and against the Bill shall be entered on the Journal of each House respectively. If any Bill shall not be returned by the President within ten Days (Sundays excepted) after it shall have been presented to him, the Same shall be a Law, in like Manner as if he had signed it, unless the Congress by their Adjournment prevent its Return, in which Case it shall not be a Law.

3. Every Order, Resolution, or Vote to which the Concurrence of the Senate and House of Representatives may be necessary (except on a question of Adjournment) shall be presented to the President of the United States; and before the Same shall take Effect, shall be approved by him, or being disapproved by him, shall be repassed by two thirds of the Senate and House of Representatives, according to the Rules and Limitations prescribed in the Case of a Bill.

Section 8

The Congress shall have power:

1. To lay and collect Taxes, Duties, Imposts and Excises, to pay the Debts and provide for the common Defence and general Welfare of the United States; but all duties, imposts and excises shall be uniform throughout the United States;

2. To borrow Money on the credit of the United States;

3. To regulate Commerce with foreign Nations, and among the several States, and with the Indian Tribes;

4. To establish a uniform Rule of Naturalization, and uniform Laws on the subject of Bankruptcies throughout the United States;

5. To coin Money, regulate the Value thereof, and of foreign Coin, and fix the Standard of Weights and Measures;

6. To provide for the Punishment of counterfeiting the Securities and current Coin of the United States;

7. To establish Post Offices and post Roads;

8. To promote the Progress of Science and useful Arts, by securing for limited Times to Authors and Inventors the exclusive Right to their respective Writings and Discoveries;

9. To constitute Tribunals inferior to the Supreme Court;

10. To define and punish Piracies and Felonies committed on the high Seas, and Offenses against the Law of Nations;

11. To declare War, grant Letters of Marque and Reprisal, and make Rules concerning Captures on Land and Water;

12. To raise and support Armies, but no Appropriation of Money to that Use shall be for a longer Term than two Years;

13. To provide and maintain a Navy;

14. To make Rules for the Government and Regulation of the land and naval Forces;

15. To provide for calling forth the Militia to execute the Laws of the Union, suppress Insurrections and repel Invasions;

16. To provide for organizing, arming, and disciplining the Militia, and for governing such Part of them as may be employed in the Service of the United States, reserving to the States respectively, the Appointment of the Officers, and the Authority of training the Militia according to the discipline prescribed by Congress;

17. To exercise exclusive Legislation in all Cases whatsoever, over such District (not exceeding ten Miles square) as may, by Session of particular States, and the Acceptance of Congress, become the Seat of the Government of the United States, and to exercise like Authority over all Places purchased by the Consent of the Legislature of the State in which the Same shall be, for the Erection of Forts, Magazines, Arsenals, dock-Yards and other needful Buildings; and

18. To make all Laws which shall be necessary and proper for carrying into Execution the foregoing Powers, and all other Powers vested by this Constitution in the Government of the United States, or in any Department or Officer thereof.

Section 9

1. The Migration or Importation of such Persons as any of the States now existing shall think proper to admit, shall not be prohibited by the Congress prior to the Year one thousand eight hundred and eight, but a Tax or duty may be imposed on such Importation, not exceeding ten dollars for each Person.

2. The Privilege of the Writ of Habeas Corpus shall not be suspended, unless when in Cases of Rebellion or Invasion the public Safety may require it.

3. No Bill of Attainder or ex post facto Law shall be passed.

4. [No Capitation, or other direct, Tax shall be laid, unless in Proportion to the Census or Enumeration herein before directed to be taken.][5]

5. No Tax or Duty shall be laid on Articles exported from any State.

6. No Preference shall be given by any Regulation of Commerce or Revenue to the Ports of one State over those of another; nor shall Vessels bound to, or from, one State, be obliged to enter, clear, or pay Duties in another.

7. No Money shall be drawn from the Treasury, but in Consequence of Appropriations made by Law; and a regular Statement and Account of the Receipts and Expenditures of all public Money shall be published from time to time.

8. No Title of Nobility shall be granted by the United States: And no Person holding any Office of Profit or Trust under them, shall, without the Consent of the Congress, accept of any present, Emolument, Office, or Title, of any kind whatever, from any King, Prince, or foreign State.

Section 10

1. No State shall enter into any Treaty, Alliance, or Confederation; grant Letters of Marque and Reprisal; coin Money; emit Bills of Credit; make any Thing but gold and silver Coin a Tender in Payment of Debts; pass any Bill of Attainder, ex post facto Law, or Law impairing the Obligation of Contracts, or grant any Title of Nobility.

2. No State shall, without the Consent of the Congress, lay any Imposts or Duties on Imports or Exports, except what may be absolutely necessary for executing its inspection Laws: and the net Produce of all Duties and Imposts, laid by any State on Imports or Exports, shall be for the Use of the Treasury of the United States; and all such Laws shall be subject to the Revision and Control of the Congress.

3. No State shall, without the Consent of Congress, lay any Duty of Tonnage, keep Troops, or Ships of War in time of Peace, enter into any Agreement or Compact with another State, or with a foreign Power, or engage in War, unless actually invaded, or in such imminent Danger as will not admit of delay.

---

[5] Changed by the Sixteenth Amendment.

ARTICLE II

Section I

1. The executive Power shall be vested in a President of the United States of America. He shall hold his Office during the Term of four Years, and, together with the Vice President, chosen for the same Term, be elected, as follows.

2. Each State shall appoint, in such Manner as the Legislature thereof may direct, a Number of Electors, equal to the whole Number of Senators and Representatives to which the State may be entitled in the Congress: but no Senator or Representative, or Person holding an Office of Trust or Profit under the United States, shall be appointed an Elector.

3. [The Electors shall meet in their respective states, and vote by Ballot for two Persons, of whom one at least shall not be an Inhabitant of the same State with themselves. And they shall make a List of all the Persons voted for, and of the Number of Votes for each; which List they shall sign and certify, and transmit sealed to the Seat of the Government of the United States, directed to the President of the Senate. The President of the Senate shall, in the Presence of the Senate and House of Representatives, open all the Certificates, and the Votes shall then be counted. The Person having the greatest Number of Votes shall be the President, if such Number be a Majority of the whole Number of Electors appointed; and if there be more than one who have such Majority, and have an equal Number of Votes, then the

   House of Representatives shall immediately choose by Ballot one of them for President; and if no Person have a Majority, then from the five highest on the List the said House shall in like manner choose the President. But in choosing the President, the Votes shall be taken by States, the Representation from each State having one Vote; A quorum for this Purpose shall consist of a Member or Members from two thirds of the States, and a Majority of all the States shall be necessary to a Choice. In every Case, after the Choice of the President, the Person having the greatest Number of Votes of the Electors shall be the Vice President. But if there should remain two or more who have equal Votes, the Senate shall choose from them by Ballot the Vice President.][6]

4. The Congress may determine the Time of choosing the Electors, and the day on which they shall give their Votes; which Day shall be the same throughout the United States.

5. No Person except a natural born Citizen, or a Citizen of the United States at the time of the Adoption of this Constitution, shall be eligible to the Office of the President; neither shall any person be eligible to that Office who shall not have attained to the Age of thirty five Years, and been fourteen Years a Resident within the United States.

6. [In Case of the Removal of the President from Office, or of his Death, Resignation, or Inability to discharge the Powers and Duties of the said Office, the Same shall devolve on the Vice President, and the Congress may by Law provide for the Case of Removal, Death, Resignation or Inability, both of the President and Vice President, declaring what Officer shall then act as President, and such Officer shall act accordingly, until the Disability be removed, or a President shall be elected.][7]

---

[6] Changed by the Twelfth Amendment.
[7] Changed by the Twenty-fifth Amendment.

7. The President shall, at stated Times, receive for his Services, a Compensation, which shall neither be increased nor diminished during the Period for which he shall have been elected, and he shall not receive within that Period any other Emolument from the United States, or any of them.

8. Before he enter the Execution of his Office, he shall take the following Oath or Affirmation:—"I do solemnly swear (or affirm) that I will faithfully execute the Office of President of the United States, and will to the best of my ability, preserve, protect, and defend the Constitution of the United States."

Section 2

1. The President shall be Commander in Chief of the Army and Navy of the United States, and of the Militia of the several States, when called into the actual Service of the United States; he may require the Opinion, in writing, of the principal Officer in each of the executive Departments, upon any Subject relating to the Duties of their respective Offices, and he shall have Power to grant Reprieves and Pardons for Offenses against the United States, except in Cases of Impeachment.

2. He shall have Power, by and with the Advice and Consent of the Senate, to make Treaties, provided two thirds of the Senators present concur; and he shall nominate, and by and with the Advice and Consent of the Senate, shall appoint Ambassadors, other public Ministers and Consuls, Judges of the supreme Court, and all other Officers of the United States, whose Appointments are not herein otherwise provided for, and which shall be established by Law; but the Congress may by Law vest the Appointment of such inferior Officers, as they think proper, in the President alone, in the Courts of Law, or in the Heads of Departments.

3. The President shall have Power to fill up all Vacancies that may happen during the Recess of the Senate, by granting Commissions which shall expire at the End of their next Session.

Section 3

He shall from time to time give to the Congress Information of the State of the Union, and recommend to their Consideration such Measures as he shall judge necessary and expedient; he may, on extraordinary Occasions, convene both Houses, or either of them, and in Case of Disagreement between them, with Respect to the Time of Adjournment, he may adjourn them to such Time as he shall think proper; he shall receive Ambassadors and other public Ministers; he shall take Care that the Laws be faithfully executed, and shall Commission all the Officers of the United States.

Section 4

The President, Vice President and all civil Officers of the United States, shall be removed from Office on Impeachment for, and Conviction of, Treason, Bribery, or other high Crimes and Misdemeanors.

ARTICLE III

Section I

The judicial Power of the United States, shall be vested in one supreme Court, and in such inferior Courts as the Congress may from time to time ordain and establish. The Judges, both of the supreme and inferior Courts, shall hold their Offices during good Behavior, and shall, at stated Times, receive for their Services a Compensation, which shall not be diminished during their Continuance in Office.

Section 2

1. The judicial Power shall extend to all Cases, in Law and Equity, arising under this Constitution, the Laws of the United States, and Treaties made, or which shall be made, under their Authority;—to all Cases affecting Ambassadors, other public Ministers and Consuls;—to all Cases of admiralty and maritime Jurisdiction;—to Controversies to which the United States shall be a Party; to Controversies between two or more States; [between a State and Citizens of another State;] between Citizens of different States; between Citizens of the same State claiming Lands under Grants of different States; [and between a State, or the Citizens thereof, and foreign States, Citizens or Subjects.][8]

2. In all Cases affecting Ambassadors, other public Ministers and Consuls, and those in which a State shall be Party, the supreme Court shall have original Jurisdiction. In all the other Cases before mentioned, the supreme Court shall have appellate Jurisdiction, both as to Law and Fact, with such Exceptions, and under such Regulations as the Congress shall make.

3. The Trial of all Crimes, except in Cases of Impeachment, shall be by Jury; and such Trial shall be held in the State where said Crimes shall have been committed; but when not committed within any State, the Trial shall be at such Place or Places as the Congress may by Law have directed.

Section 3

1. Treason against the United States shall consist only in levying War against them, or in adhering to their Enemies, giving them Aid and Comfort. No Person shall be convicted of Treason unless on the Testimony of two Witnesses to the same overt Act, or on Confession in open Court.

2. The Congress shall have Power to declare the Punishment of Treason, but no Attainder of Treason shall work Corruption of Blood, or Forfeiture except during the Life of the Person attainted.

ARTICLE IV

Section 1

Full Faith and Credit shall be given in each State to the public Acts, Records, and judicial Proceedings of every other State; And the Congress may by general Laws prescribe the manner in which such Acts, Records and Proceedings shall be proved, and the Effect thereof.

Section 2

1. The Citizens of each State shall be entitled to all Privileges and Immunities of Citizens in the several States.

2. A Person charged in any State with Treason, Felony, or other Crime, who shall flee from Justice, and be found in another State, shall on Demand of the executive Authority of the State from which he fled, be delivered up, to be removed to the State having Jurisdiction of the Crime.

3. [No person held to Service or Labour in one State, under the Laws thereof, escaping into another, shall, in Consequence of any Law or Regulation therein, be discharged from such Service or

---

[8] Changed by the Eleventh Amendment.

Labour, but shall be delivered up on Claim of the Party to whom such Service or Labour may be due.][9]

Section 3

1. New States may be admitted by the Congress into this Union; but no new State shall be formed or erected within the Jurisdiction of any other State; nor any State be formed by the Junction of two or more States, or parts of States, without the Consent of the Legislatures of the States concerned as well as of the Congress.

2. The Congress shall have Power to dispose of and make all needful Rules and Regulations respecting the territory or other Property belonging to the United States; and nothing in this Constitution shall be so construed as to Prejudice any Claims of the United States, or of any particular State.

Section 4

The United States shall guarantee to every State in this Union a Republican Form of Government, and shall protect each of them against Invasion; and on Application of the Legislature, or of the Executive (when the Legislature cannot be convened) against domestic Violence.

ARTICLE V

The Congress, whenever two thirds of both Houses shall deem it necessary, shall propose Amendments to this Constitution, or, on the Application of the Legislatures of two thirds of the several States, shall call a Convention for proposing Amendments, which, in either Case, shall be valid to all Intents and Purposes, as Part of this Constitution, when ratified by the Legislatures of three fourths of the several States, or by Conventions in three fourths thereof, as the one or the other Mode of Ratification may be proposed by the Congress; Provided that no Amendment which may be made prior to the Year One thousand eight hundred and eight shall in any Manner affect the first and fourth Clauses in the Ninth Section of the first Article; and that no State, without its Consent, shall be deprived of its equal Suffrage in the Senate.

ARTICLE VI

1. All debts contracted and Engagements entered into, before the Adoption of this Constitution, shall be as valid against the United States under this Constitution, as under the Confederation.

2. This Constitution, and the Laws of the United States which shall be made in Pursuance thereof, and all Treaties made, or which shall be made, under the Authority of the United States, shall be the supreme Law of the Land; and the Judges in every State shall be bound thereby, any Thing in the Constitution or Laws of any State to the Contrary notwithstanding.

3. The Senators and Representatives before mentioned, and the Members of the several State Legislatures, and all executive and judicial Officers, both of the United States and of the several States, shall be bound by Oath or Affirmation, to support this Constitution; but no religious Test shall ever be required as a Qualification to any Office or public Trust under the United States.

---

[9] Changed by the Thirteenth Amendment.

ARTICLE VII

The Ratification of the Conventions of nine States, shall be sufficient for the Establishment of this Constitution between the States so ratifying the Same.

Done in Convention by the unanimous consent of the States present the seventeenth day of September in the year of our Lord one thousand seven hundred and eighty seven and of the Independence of the United States of America the Twelfth. In witness whereof we have hereunto subscribed our Names,

George Washington—President
and deputy from Virginia

(This Constitution was adopted on September 17, 1787 by the Constitutional Convention, and was declared ratified on July 2, 1788)

Signers of the Constitution

New-Hampshire
John Langdon
Nicholas Gilman

Massachusetts
Nathaniel Gorham
Rufus King

Connecticut
William Samuel Johnson
Roger Sherman

New York
Alexander Hamilton

New Jersey
William Livingston
David Brearley
William Paterson
Jonathan Dayton

Pennsylvania
Benjamin Franklin
Thomas Mifflin
Robert Morris
George Clymer
Thomas Fitzsimons
Jared Ingersoll
James Wilson
Gouverneur Morris

Delaware
George Read
Gunning Bedford, Jr.
John Dickinson
Richard Bassett
Jacob Broom

Maryland
James McHenry
Daniel of St. Tho. Jenifer
Daniel Carroll

Virginia
John Blair
James Madison, Junior

North Carolina
William Blount
Richard Dobbs Spaight
Hugh Williamson

South Carolina
John Ruthledge
Charles Cotesworth Pinckney
Charles Pinckney
Pierce Butler

Georgia
William Few
Abraham Baldwin

Attest: William Jackson, Secretary

AMENDMENTS TO THE CONSTITUTION
OF THE UNITED STATES OF AMERICA

AMENDMENT I

Congress shall make no law respecting an establishment of religion, or prohibiting the free exercise thereof, or abridging the freedom of speech, or of the press, or the right of the people peaceably to assemble, and to petition the Government for a redress of grievances. (Ratified December, 1791.)

AMENDMENT II

A well regulated Militia, being necessary to the security of a free State, the right of the people to keep and bear Arms, shall not be infringed. (Ratified December, 1791.)

AMENDMENT III

No Soldier shall, in time of peace be quartered in any house, without the consent of the Owner, nor in time of war, but in a manner to be prescribed by law. (Ratified December, 1791.)

AMENDMENT IV

The right of the people to be secure in their persons, houses, papers, and effects, against unreasonable searches and seizures, shall not be violated, and no Warrants shall issue, but upon probable cause, supported by Oath or affirmation, and particularly describing the place to be searched, and the persons or things to be seized. (Ratified December, 1791.)

AMENDMENT V

No person shall be held to answer for a capital, or otherwise infamous crime, unless on a presentment or indictment of a Grand Jury, except in cases arising in the land or naval forces, or in the Militia, when in actual service in time of War or public danger; nor shall any person be subject for the same offence to be twice put in jeopardy of life or limb, nor shall be compelled in any criminal case to be a witness against himself, nor be deprived of life, liberty, or property, without due process of law; nor shall private property be taken for public use without just compensation. (Ratified December, 1791.)

AMENDMENT VI

In all criminal prosecutions, the accused shall enjoy the right to a speedy and public trial, by an impartial jury of the State and district wherein the crime shall have been committed; which district shall have been previously ascertained by law, and to be informed of the nature and cause of the accusation; to be confronted with the witnesses against him; to have compulsory process for obtaining witnesses in his favor, and to have the assistance of counsel for his defence. (Ratified December, 1791.)

AMENDMENT VII

In Suits at common law, where the value in controversy shall exceed twenty dollars, the right of trial by jury shall be preserved, and no fact tried by a jury shall be otherwise re-examined in any Court of the United States, than according to the rules of the common law. (Ratified December, 1791.)

AMENDMENT VIII

Excessive bail shall not be required, nor excessive fines imposed, nor cruel and unusual punishments inflicted. (Ratified December, 1791.)

AMENDMENT IX

The enumeration in the Constitution of certain rights shall not be construed to deny or disparage others retained by the people. (Ratified December, 1791.)

AMENDMENT X

The powers not delegated to the United States by the Constitution, nor prohibited by it to the States, are reserved to the States respectively, or to the people. (Ratified December, 1791.)

AMENDMENT XI

The Judicial power of the United States shall not be construed to extend to any suit in law or equity, commenced or prosecuted against one of the United States by Citizens of another State, or by Citizens or Subjects of any Foreign State. (Ratified February, 1795.)

AMENDMENT XII

The Electors shall meet in their respective states, and vote by ballot for President and Vice President, one of whom, at least, shall not be an inhabitant of the same state with themselves; they shall name in their ballots the person voted for as President, and in distinct ballots the person voted for as Vice-President, and they shall make distinct lists of all persons voted for as President, and of all persons voted for as Vice-President, and of the number of votes for each, which lists they shall sign and certify, and transmit sealed to the seat of the government of the United States, directed to the President of the Senate;—The President of the Senate shall, in the presence of the Senate and House of Representatives, open all the certificates and the votes shall then be counted;—The person having the greatest number of votes for President, shall be the President, if such number be a majority of the whole number of Electors appointed; and if no person have such majority, then from the persons having the highest numbers not exceeding three on the list of those voted for as President, the House of Representatives shall choose immediately, by ballot, the President. But in choosing the President, the votes shall be taken by states, the representation from each state having one vote; a quorum for this purpose shall consist of a member or members from two-thirds of the states, and a majority of all the states shall be necessary to a choice. [And if the House of Representatives shall not choose a President whenever the right of choice shall devolve upon them, before the fourth day of March next following, then the Vice-President shall act as President, as in the case of the death or other constitutional disability of the President—][1] The person having the greatest number of votes as Vice-President, shall be the Vice-President, if such number be a majority of the whole number of Electors appointed, and if no person have a majority, then from the two highest numbers on the list, the Senate shall choose the Vice-President; a quorum for the purpose shall consist of two-thirds of the whole number of Senators, and a majority of the whole number shall be necessary to a choice. But no person constitutionally ineligible to the office of President shall be eligible to that of Vice-President of the United States. (Ratified June, 1804.)

---

[1] Superseded by Section 3 of the Twentieth Amendment.

AMENDMENT XIII

Section 1

Neither slavery nor involuntary servitude, except as a punishment for crime whereof the party shall have been duly convicted, shall exist within the United States, or any place subject to their jurisdiction.

Section 2

Congress shall have power to enforce this article by appropriate legislation. (Ratified December, 1865.)

AMENDMENT XIV

Section 1

All persons born or naturalized in the United States and subject to the jurisdiction thereof, are citizens of the United States and of the State wherein they reside. No State shall make or enforce any law which shall abridge the privileges or immunities of citizens of the United States; nor shall any State deprive any person of life, liberty, or property, without due process of law; nor deny to any person within its jurisdiction the equal protection of the laws.

Section 2

Representatives shall be apportioned among the several States according to their respective numbers, counting the whole number of persons in each State, excluding Indians not taxed. But when the right to vote at any election for the choice of electors for President and Vice President of the United States, Representatives in Congress, the Executive and Judicial officers of a State, or the members of the Legislature thereof, is denied to any of the male inhabitants of such State, being twenty-one years of age, and citizens of the United States, or in any way abridged, except for participation in rebellion, or other crime, the basis of representation therein shall be reduced in the proportion which the number of such male citizens shall bear to the whole number of male citizens twenty-one years of age in such State.

Section 3

No person shall be a Senator or a Representative in Congress, or elector of President and Vice President, or hold any office, civil or military, under the United States, or under any State, who, having previously taken an oath, as a member of Congress, or as an officer of the United States, or as a member of any State legislature, or as an executive or judicial officer of any State, to support the Constitution of the United States, shall have engaged in insurrection or rebellion against the same, or given aid or comfort to the enemies thereof. But Congress may by a vote of two-thirds of each House, remove such disability.

Section 4

The validity of the public debt of the United States, authorized by law, including debts incurred for payment of pensions and bounties for services in suppressing insurrection or rebellion, shall not be questioned. But neither the United States nor any State shall assume or pay any debt or obligation incurred in aid of insurrection or rebellion against the United States, or any claim for the loss or emancipation of any slave; but all such debts, obligations and claims shall be held illegal and void.

Section 5

The Congress shall have power to enforce, by appropriate legislation, the provisions of this article. (Ratified July, 1868.)

AMENDMENT XV

Section 1

The right of citizens of the United States to vote shall not be denied or abridged by the United States or by any State on account of race, color, or previous condition of servitude.

Section 2

The Congress shall have power to enforce this article by appropriate legislation. (Ratified February, 1870.)

AMENDMENT XVI

The Congress shall have power to lay and collect taxes on incomes, from whatever source derived, without apportionment among the several States, and without regard to any census or enumeration. (Ratified February, 1913.)

AMENDMENT XVII

The Senate of the United States shall be composed of two Senators from each State, elected by the people thereof, for six years; and each Senator shall have one vote. The electors in each State shall have the qualifications requisite for electors of the most numerous branch of the State legislatures.

When vacancies happen in the representation of any State in the Senate, the executive authority of such State shall issue writs of election to fill such vacancies: Provided, That the legislature of any State may empower the executive thereof to make temporary appointments until the people fill the vacancies by election as the legislature may direct.

This amendment shall not be so construed as to affect the election or term of any Senator chosen before it becomes valid as part of the Constitution. (Ratified April, 1913.)

AMENDMENT XVIII

Section 1

After one year from the ratification of this article the manufacture, sale, or transportation of intoxicating liquors within, the importation thereof into, or the exportation thereof from the United States and all territory subject to the jurisdiction thereof for beverage purposes is hereby prohibited.

Section 2

The Congress and the several States shall have concurrent power to enforce this article by appropriate legislation.

Section 3

This article shall be inoperative unless it shall have been ratified as an amendment to the Constitution by the legislatures of the several States, as provided in the Constitution, within seven years from the date of the submission hereof to the States by the Congress.][2] (Ratified January, 1919.)

AMENDMENT XIX

The right of citizens of the United States to vote shall not be denied or abridged by the United States or by any State on account of sex.

Congress shall have power to enforce this article by appropriate legislation. (Ratified August, 1920.)

AMENDMENT XX

Section 1

The terms of the President and Vice President shall end at noon on the 20th day of January, and the terms of Senators and Representatives at noon on the 3d day of January, of the years in which such terms would have ended if this article had not been ratified; and the terms of their successors shall then begin.

Section 2

The Congress shall assemble at least once in every year, and such meeting shall begin at noon on the 3d day of January, unless they shall by law appoint a different day.

Section 3

If, at the time fixed for the beginning of the term of the President, the President elect shall have died, the Vice President elect shall become President. If a President shall not have been chosen before the time fixed for the beginning of his term, or if the President elect shall have failed to qualify, then the Vice President elect shall act as President until a President shall have qualified; and the Congress may by law provide for the case wherein neither a President elect nor a Vice President elect shall have qualified, declaring who shall then act as President, or the manner in which one who is to act shall be selected, and such person shall act accordingly until a President or Vice President shall have qualified.

Section 4

The Congress may by law provide for the case of the death of any of the persons from whom the House of Representatives may choose a President whenever the right of choice shall have devolved upon them, and for the case of the death of any of the persons from whom the Senate may choose a Vice President whenever the right of choice shall have devolved upon them.

Section 5

Sections I and 2 shall take effect on the 15th day of October following the ratification of this article.

---

[2] Repealed by the Twenty-first Amendment.

Section 6

This article shall be inoperative unless it shall have been ratified as an amendment to the Constitution by the legislatures of three-fourths of the several States within seven years from the date of its submission. (Ratified January, 1933.)

AMENDMENT XXI

Section 1

The eighteenth article of amendment to the Constitution of the United States is hereby repealed.

Section 2

The transportation or importation into any State, Territory, or possession of the United States for delivery or use therein of intoxicating liquors, in violation of the laws thereof, is hereby prohibited.

Section 3

This article shall be inoperative unless it shall have been ratified as an amendment to the Constitution by conventions in the several States, as provided in the Constitution, within seven years from the date of the submission hereof to the States by the Congress. (Ratified December, 1933.)

AMENDMENT XXII

Section I

No person shall be elected to the office of the President more than twice, and no person who has held the office of President, or acted as President, for more than two years of a term to which some other person was elected President shall be elected to the office of the President more than once. But this Article shall not apply to any person holding the office of President when this Article was proposed by the Congress, and shall not prevent any person who may be holding the office of President, or acting as President, during the term within which this Article becomes operative from holding the office of President or acting as President during the remainder of such term.

Section 2

This article shall be inoperative unless it shall have been ratified as an amendment to the Constitution by the legislatures of three-fourths of the several States within seven years from the date of its submission to the States by the Congress. (Ratified February, 1951.)

AMENDMENT XXIII

Section 1

The District constituting the seat of Government of the United States shall appoint in such manner as the Congress may direct:

A number of electors of President and Vice President equal to the whole number of Senators and Representatives in Congress to which the District would be entitled if it were a State, but in no event more than the least populous State; they shall be in addition to those appointed by the States, but they shall be considered, for the purposes of the election of President and Vice President, to be electors appointed by a State; and they shall meet in the District and perform such duties as provided by the twelfth article of amendment.

Section 2

The Congress shall have power to enforce this article by appropriate legislation. (Ratified March, 1961.)

AMENDMENT XXIV

Section 1

The right of citizens of the United States to vote in any primary or other election for President or Vice President, for electors for President or Vice President, or for Senator or Representative in Congress, shall not be denied or abridged by the United States or any State by reason of failure to pay any poll tax or other tax.

Section 2

The Congress shall have power to enforce this article by appropriate legislation. (Ratified January, 1964.)

AMENDMENT XXV

Section 1

In case of the removal of the President from office or of his death or resignation, the Vice President shall become President.

Section 2

Whenever there is a vacancy in the office of the Vice President, the President shall nominate a Vice President who shall take office upon confirmation by a majority vote of both Houses of Congress.

Section 3

Whenever the President transmits to the President pro tempore of the Senate and the Speaker of the House of Representatives his written declaration that he is unable to discharge the powers and duties of his office, and until he transmits to them a written declaration to the contrary, such powers and duties shall be discharged by the Vice President as Acting President.

Section 4

Whenever the Vice President and a majority of either the principal officers of the executive departments or of such other body as Congress may by law provide, transmit to the President pro tempore of the Senate and the Speaker of the House of Representatives their written declaration that the President is unable to discharge the powers and duties of his office, the Vice President shall immediately assume the powers and duties of the office as Acting President.

Thereafter, when the President transmits to the President pro tempore of the Senate and the Speaker of the House of Representatives his written declaration that no inability exists, he shall resume the powers and duties of his office unless the Vice President and a majority of either the principal officers of the executive department or of such other body as Congress may by law provide, transmit within four days to the President pro tempore of the Senate and the Speaker of the House of Representatives their written declaration that the President is unable to discharge the powers and duties of his office. Thereupon Congress shall decide the issue, assembling within forty-eight hours for that purpose if not in session. If the Congress, within twenty-one days after receipt of the latter written declaration, or, if Congress is not in session, within twenty-one days after Congress is required to assemble, determines by two-thirds vote of both Houses that the President is unable to discharge the powers and duties of his office, the Vice President shall continue to discharge the same as Acting President; otherwise, the President shall resume the powers and duties of his office. (Ratified February, 1967.)

AMENDMENT XXVI

Section I

The right of citizens of the United States, who are eighteen years of age or older, to vote shall not be denied or abridged by the United States or by any State on account of age.

Section 2

The Congress shall have power to enforce this article by appropriate legislation. (Ratified July, 1971.)

AMENDMENT XXVII

No law varying the compensation for the services of the Senators or Representatives, shall take effect, until an election of Representatives shall have intervened. (Ratified May, 1992.)

8 Rules of the Game

Remember Anwar Khalil's Story (pp. 4 and 5)

1. Anwar Khalil to judge
2. Katherine Morrison to TV audience
3. Marilyn Corbin to jury
4. Barbara Weaver to Marilyn Corbin
5. Marilyn Corbin to jury

a. 4   b. 5   c. 1   d. 2   e. 3

1. alibi
2. justice
3. victim
4. verdict
5. circumstantial evidence
6. acquitted

Answers may vary. Here are some possible answers.

1. I feel wonderful.
2. Barbara Weaver's testimony convinced them.
3. It gave me a new trial when new evidence was discovered.
4. If you are innocent, don't stop trying to prove it.

Remember the Police Officers' Story (pp. 6 and 7)

1. Brenda to Diane Clayton
2. Dave Kinnard to Mayor Reilly and Derek Powell
3. Phil Genelli to Frankie
4. Sandra Baker to Phil Genelli
5. Phil Genelli to Sandra Baker

a. 5   b. 1   c. 6   d. 3   e. 4   f. 2

1. evidence
2. illegal search
3. charges
4. perjury
5. arrests
6. testifies

Answers may vary. Here are some possible answers.

1. In a court of law, I must tell the truth.
2. Then you should have followed the proper procedures.
3. Even criminals have the right to due process.
4. I know we performed an illegal search.

Remember Turning Points (pp. 8 and 9)

1. T   2. F   3. F   4. T   5. F

Content

1. the kind of work people do
2. what people believe
3. where people choose to live
4. the people they choose as friends

Procedures

1. conducting hearings
2. enforcing the law
3. investigating crimes
4. trying people charged with crimes

 Answers may vary. Here are some possible answers.

1. People are free to worship whatever god they choose, or no god at all.
2. Qualified people cannot be unfairly prevented from getting a job or promotion.
3. Laws cannot prevent people of one race or religion from living in a neighborhood or building.
4. Laws cannot restrict a person's choice of friends or associates.
5. Police cannot search property without permission of the owner or without a search warrant.
6. Courts cannot allow evidence that was obtained illegally to be used in a trial.

Making Connections (p. 9)

1. Frankie and Nick (1 point); Anwar Khalil (1 point)
2. possession of drugs with intent to sell (1 point); an ATM robbery (1 point)

1. The image of the robber caught by a closed-circuit camera looked like Anwar Khalil. The victim picked Khalil out of a lineup of possible suspects. (1 point)
   They tricked Frankie and Nick by saying the brake light didn't work and used that as an excuse to look into the car, where they found illegal drugs. (1 point)
2. The court granted Anwar Khalil a new trial because of new evidence—a witness, Barbara Weaver, who could verify where Khalil was at the time of the robbery. (1 point); The court did not allow the drugs found in Frankie and Nick's car to be admitted as evidence because the evidence was obtained without a search warrant. (1 point)

 Answers may vary. Here are some possible answers.

1. They need to be more thorough in their investigation. If a witness they didn't question turns up later, their case may be overturned. (1 point)

2. They need to follow due process procedures if they expect evidence to be used in court. If the evidence is not useable, they may not get a conviction. (1 point)

Find Out More: Key Ideas (p. 12)

1. **b.** *Due process* means that the content of laws that legislatures pass must be fair and reasonable.
2. **c.** They were added when the first ten amendments, called the Bill of Rights, were approved.
3. **a.** The Fifth Amendment was designed to protect people from unfair and unreasonable treatment by the federal government.
4. **a.** Government is responsible for protecting the rights of all people, even people who have broken the law and endangered the lives, liberty, or property of others.

 Answers may vary. Here are some possible answers.

1. all procedures and methods used to enforce the law must be fair and reasonable.
2. the type of evidence and testimony that can be presented, how the police can obtain evidence, and how attorneys can challenge testimony.

Answers may vary. Here are some possible answers.

1. The Supreme Court has thrown out laws that allowed the government to unfairly control individual freedoms, such as the use of contraceptives by married couples.
2. The freedom to believe what I want, live where I like, choose the work I do, choose the friends I have.

Inside Information (p. 14)

```
A  S  P  C  O  N  S  T  I  T  U  T  I  O  N
R  I  P  L  F  A  T  O  R  H  C  B  L  I  U
K  J  O  P  T  O  M  E  E  I  G  H  T  P  G
S  U  P  R  E  M  E  D  J  Q  U  E  I  N  Y
H  S  R  E  L  V  X  C  G  T  F  M  B  E  S
A  T  L  S  F  E  R  N  R  P  D  C  B  E  F
L  I  M  I  H  A  P  P  E  A  L  S  T  T  Q
T  C  P  D  N  C  L  R  T  U  G  A  F  H  U
R  E  M  E  A  Q  R  D  I  E  T  B  V  A  S
T  S  E  N  A  T  E  L  R  S  C  A  R  E  S
I  T  N  T  T  L  N  A  E  T  C  U  S  R  A
```

1. Supreme
2. justices
3. chief
4. eight
5. president, Senate
6. retire, die
7. appeals
8. Constitution, states

9 Sticks and Stones, Part 1

Remember the Story (pp. 18 and 19)

1. Edward Tarkowitz to Rick Jensen
2. Scooter Harrison to Rick Jensen
3. Rick Jensen to Scooter Harrison
4. Lawrence Hamilton to Mike Murdock
5. Mr. Hadim to Edward Tarkowitz
6. Mike Murdock to Mrs. Jensen

a. 5   b. 3   c. 1   d. 4   e. 2

1. assault and battery   3. Miranda rights   5. cross-examine
2. harass   4. convict

Answers may vary. Here are some possible answers.

1. I was afraid he would hurt me or a member of my family.
2. I cannot live with fear forever.
3. I will tell the truth.
4. The jury will listen to the facts. The law protects everyone.

Remember Turning Points (pp. 20 and 21)

1. F   2. F   3. T   4. T   5. F

Under due process, law enforcement officials are expected to: 2,   3,   6

Under due process, law enforcement officials cannot: 1,   4,   5

1. The detectives cannot charge Rick Jensen without solid evidence.
2. Rick Jensen cannot be convicted without a trial.
3. The jury cannot convict Rick Jensen without proving that he committed the crime. He also cannot be convicted of a crime without the following due process procedures:
   • the right to know the charges against him
   • the right to a speedy and public trial
   • the right to an impartial jury
   • the right to be defended by legal counsel
   • the right to force witnesses to appear in court
   • the right to cross-examine witnesses

Making Connections (p. 21)

Rick Jensen (1 point)

Edward Tarkowitz (1 point)

Detectives Murdock and Burrows (1 point)

🔔 🔔 assault and battery (1 point)

after the detectives found a ring in Rick Jensen's room that was missing a stone, and the colored stone found at the crime scene fit the ring (2 points)

🔔 🔔 🔔 Yes, in several ways: (1) they read him the Miranda rights; (2) they allowed him to have an attorney present when he was questioned; and (3) they didn't charge him with a crime until they had solid evidence. (3 points)

Yes, the detectives did not have a search warrant that would allow them to search for items such as the ring that were not in plain sight. (1 point)

Find Out More: Key Ideas (p. 24)

🔔 1. **b.** In the United States, people accused of crimes are assumed to be innocent until proven guilty.
2. **c.** Due process is the right to be treated fairly by government.
3. **c.** People cannot be held in jail unless they are charged with a crime and given a trial.
4. **b.** People cannot be searched or their property taken without a warrant.

🔔 🔔 Answers may vary. Here are some possible answers.

1. during the colonial period many colonists lost their individual rights to life, liberty, and property. If the men who wrote the Constitution didn't establish due process protections for people accused of crimes, they knew that governments could take away these individual rights.
2. the right to know the crime he is accused of; the right to a quick, public trial; the right to have an impartial jury; the right to have a lawyer; the right to make witnesses come to court to testify; and the right to question any witness.

🔔 🔔 🔔 Answers may vary. Here are some possible answers.

1. People accused of crimes have the right to a trial.
   - In a trial, the government must present evidence to prove that a person is guilty of a crime.
   - In a trial, the person accused of a crime has the right to have a lawyer to represent him.
   - The lawyer can present evidence to show that the accused is innocent.
   - The trial must be public; it cannot be held in secret.
   - The law says that any punishment for a crime must be fair and reasonable.
2. The answer is your personal opinion.

Inside Information (p. 26)

Coin or bill	Whose picture is on it?	Why was each person honored?
penny	Abraham Lincoln	As sixteenth president, Abraham Lincoln signed the Emancipation Proclamation that freed the slaves and led the country through a difficult period—the Civil War.
nickel	Thomas Jefferson	Thomas Jefferson drafted the Declaration of Independence and was the third president of the United States.
dime	Franklin D. Roosevelt	Franklin D. Roosevelt became president during the Great Depression, and he led the country during World War II.
quarter	George Washington	George Washington led the colonial army in the War for Independence against England and was the first president of the United States.
half-dollar	John F. Kennedy	John F. Kennedy, the popular young 35th president of the United States, was shot and killed in office in 1963.
one-dollar bill	George Washington	George Washington led the colonial army in the War for Independence against England and was the first president of the United States.
five-dollar bill	Abraham Lincoln	Abraham Lincoln signed the Emancipation Proclamation that freed the slaves and led the country through a difficult period—the Civil War.
ten-dollar bill	Alexander Hamilton	Alexander Hamilton was a statesman during the early days of the United States and first secretary of the treasury.
twenty-dollar bill	Andrew Jackson	Andrew Jackson was a military hero in the War of 1812 and a congressman who became the seventh president of the United States.
fifty-dollar bill	Ulysses S. Grant	Grant was the eighteenth president of the United States and a military leader of the Union forces during the Civil War.
one-hundred dollar bill	Benjamin Franklin	Benjamin Franklin was a statesman, inventor, and respected leader during the early days of the United States.

Answers for Exercises

10 Sticks and Stones, Part 2

Remember the Story (pp. 30 and 31)

1. Lawrence Hamilton to jury
2. Phil Burrows to Marty Siegel
3. Judge to Marty Siegel and Lawrence Hamilton
4. Mayor Reilly to Marty Siegel
5. Scooter Harrison to Marty Siegel and jury

a. 3   b. 5   c. 4   d. 2   e. 1

1. defense
2. jury
3. prosecution
4. search warrant
5. witness
6. inadmissible

Answers may vary. Here are some possible answers.

1. The detectives said that they were followiong procedures when they found the ring in Rick's bedroom.
2. He knew Jensen was wrong to hurt Tarkowitz.
3. I think they will find Jensen guilty.
4. Our case would be weak. The jury would not have enough evidence to convict Tarkowitz.

Remember Turning Points (pp. 32 and 33)

1. F   2. T   3. F   4. F   5. F

Prosecuting Attorneys	2,	3		
Both	1,	7,	8,	9
Defense Attorneys	4,	5,	6	

1. • collect evidence
   • question potential jurors
   • make opening statements
   • call witnesses
   • cross-examine witnesses called by the opposing side
   • make closing arguments

2. • has the right to have an attorney
   • can be present in courtroom
   • doesn't have to answer questions

3. • listens to the evidence
   • discusses the case once both sides have been presented
   • reaches a verdict

4. • determines whether or not evidence can be used
   • determines punishment of accused if found guilty
   • rules on objection raised by defense or prosecution

Making Connections (p. 33)

Assistant District Attorney Marty Siegel (1 point)

Lawrence Hamilton (1 point)

There were three pieces of evidence: (1) shoes that matched shoe prints at the scene of the crime; (2) a ring with a missing stone; and (3) a stone found at the scene of the crime, which fit the ring. (2 points)

The judge decides that the ring and missing stone are inadmissible. Although Mrs. Jensen allowed the detectives to search her son's room, they could only use what was clearly visible as evidence. The ring was in the back of a partially opened drawer. To search the drawer would have required a search warrant. (2 points)

The judge was impartial. He didn't favor one side more than the other. (1 point)

When Jensen's attorney objected to the defense attorney's questions for Scooter Thompson, he overruled some and sustained others. (1 point)

Find Out More: Key Ideas (p. 36)

1. **c.** Mr. Suspect has the right to telephone an attorney, or someone else, before he is jailed.
2. **c.** If the evidence against Mr. Suspect is strong, the defense attorney may advise his client to plea bargain—to plead guilty in exchange for a less serious charge or a shorter sentence.
3. **b.** If Mr. Suspect doesn't return, the court keeps the bail, and a warrant is issued for his arrest.
4. **a.** The judge can dismiss the case if there is not probable cause to believe Suspect committed the crime.

Answers may vary. Here are some possible answers.

1. that people who are arrested have the right to remain silent and to have a lawyer present during questioning.
2. that there is good reason to believe that a criminal charge is supported by legally obtained evidence.

Answers may vary. Here are some possible answers.

1. • The prosecuting attorney decides the case is too weak.
   • The judge dismisses the case at a preliminary hearing.
   • The judge rules that key evidence cannot be used in a trial, and the prosecutor drops the case.
   • The defendant agrees to plead guilty in exchange for a lighter punishment.

2. • People have been held in jail although no charges have been brought against them.
   • People have been convicted of crimes without a trial by jury.
   • People have been searched and their property seized without a warrant.

Inside Information (p. 38)

1. Alaska
2. Rhode Island
3. California
4. Wyoming
5. Florida
6. Hawaii
7. Colorado
8. Texas
9. Louisiana
10. Michigan
11. Ohio
12. Alaska
13. New Jersey
14. Illinois
15. New York
16. Utah
17. Minnesota
18. Florida

11 A House Divided

Remember the Story (pp. 42 and 43)

1. Malik Williams to Crowd
2. Nate Thompson to Thompson advisor
3. Malik Williams to Derek Powell
4. Mayor Reilly to Derek Powell
5. Derek Powell to Mayor Reilly
6. Diane Clayton to Derek Powell

a. 3   b. 1   c. 4   d. 2   e. 5

1. challenger
2. election
3. administration
4. candidates
5. campaign
6. system
7. leave of absence

Answers may vary. Here are some possible answers.

1. Yes, I just needed some time off.
2. He had some good ideas
3. So do I. The Mayor depends on your support in the council.
4. I think you should listen to some of Malik Williams' ideas.

Remember Turning Points (pp. 44 and 45)

1. c   2. d   3. e   4. a   5. b

1. white males with property
2. all white males
3. black males
4. women
5. citizens 18 and over

1. black males

   As a result of the North's victory in the Civil War, slaves were freed and black males won the right to vote.

2. women

   They worked in the factories while the men were at war. After working outside the home, they felt they had earned the right to vote, and renewed efforts to get it.

3. people between 18 and 21

   If 18-year-olds were expected to fight in the war, they believed that they should be able to vote for or against the people who made the decision to go to war.

Making Connections (p. 45)

- Nate Thompson and Malik Williams (2 points)
- Nate Thompson (1 point)
- Malik Williams (1 point)

- Nate Thompson has served as a councilman for ten years. In that time he has learned to work within the political system to accomplish things for his district. Progress is often slow, but positive changes are being made. (1 point)
- Malik Williams is young and impatient. He is not willing to play the game. He demands immediate changes for the black community. (1 point)

- Nate Thompson is the winner. (1 point)
- Even though many people in the district are excited by Williams' energy and vision for the black community, they know that Thompson has done a good job as councilman. For many, voting for Thompson seemed "safer." (1 point)
- Williams may have pushed for change too hard and too quickly. (1 point)

Find Out More: Key Ideas (p. 48)

1. **b.** In a general election, voters make final decisions about candidates and issues
2. **c.** In almost every state, you must register before you vote.
3. **a.** There are two major political parties in the United States—Democrats and Republicans.
4. **a.** People generally vote in neighborhood polling places.

Answers may vary. Here are some possible answers.

1. that you must be at least 18 years old, a citizen of the United States, and a resident of the state in which you vote.

2. the votes they win can change the outcome of the election   OR
   the candidates raise issues for people to think about.

Answers may vary. Here are some possible answers.

1. A person needs to know the candidates' views on important issues, their backgrounds, and their experience.

2. • Voting is a privilege. Many countries want to be sure that the people who vote are qualified.
   - Citizens who are under age 18 cannot vote because they are not adults and are not considered old enough to vote wisely.
   - Citizens who have been convicted of a crime and are in jail or on parole cannot vote because when they are convicted of a crime, they lose their right to vote.
   - Lawful permanent residents cannot vote because they are not citizens and therefore do not have the privilege of voting.

Inside Information (p. 50)

Question	President	Senator	Representative
1. How many people can hold this office at a given time? (1, 5, 50, 100, 325, 435, 535)	1	50	435
2. If you are elected, how long is your term of office? (2, 4, 6, 8, 10, 12, 14 years)	4 years	6 years	2 years
3. How many terms can you serve? (2, 3, 4, 5, 6, no limit)	two (2)	no limit	no limit
4. What is the minimum age for each office? (20, 25, 30, 35, 40, 45, 50)	35	30	25
5. Must you have been born in the United States? (yes, no)	yes	no	no
6. Must you be a citizen of the United States? (yes, no)	yes	yes	yes
7. How long must you have lived in the United States? (3, 5, 7, 9, 10, 12, 14, 16 years)	14 years	9 years	7 years

12 Fall from Grace, Part 1

Remember the Story (pp. 54 and 55)

1. Roberto Sanchez to Diane Clayton and Jenny Tang
2. Diane Clayton to Roberto Sanchez
3. Jess Holcomb to Diane Clayton
4. Amanda Hathaway to Carla Castillo and TV audience
5. Carla Castillo to Steve Richardson
6. Steve Richardson to Carla Castillo

a. 3   b. 1   c. 5   d. 6   e. 4   f. 2

1. violation
2. documents
3. standard
4. penalties
5. allegations
6. negligent
7. comply

Answers may vary. Here are some possible answers.

- The building had outdated wiring.
- The owners are responsible.
- We can't find the owners.
- I represent their interests. I am working with City Hall to find a solution to their problems.

Remember Turning Points (pp. 56 and 57)

1. F   2. T   3. T   4. F   5. T

1. direct democracy
2. representative government
3. basic rights
4. limited government

Examples may vary. Here are some possible answers.

1. concept: direct democracy

   example: town meetings in small New England towns

2. concept: representative democracy

   example: senators and representatives in U.S. Congress and in state legislatures; members of city councils

3. concept: basic rights

   example: life, liberty, property, pursuit of happiness; trial by jury; freedom of speech

4. concept: limited government
   example: people elect their representatives for limited terms

Making Connections (p. 57)

Councilwoman Amanda Hathaway (1 point)

- can't find owners of building   OR
  don't have documentation (1 point)
- Carla Castillo (1 point)
- finds out who the owners are (1 point)

Answers may vary. Here is a possible answer.

If the owners can be found, they can be forced to fix the apartment because it is in violation of health and safety standards.

Find Out More: Key Ideas (p. 60)

1. **a.** And so they created the world's first direct democracy, a form of government in which laws are made by the people themselves.
2. **b.** State and federal legislatures, as well as many local governments in the United States, are more like the representative government of ancient Rome.
3. **b.** They forced the king to sign the Magna Carta—an agreement that gave basic rights to the nobility.
4. **b.** A government formed by the people depends on the consent of the governed—the people themselves—for its existence and its power.

Answers may vary. Here are some possible answers.

1. their votes decide who will hold power in the government.

2. government serves to protect the basic rights of the people.   OR
   government depends on the consent of the people.   OR
   the concept of limited government.

Answers may vary. Here are some possible answers.

1. The government must follow the Constitution. The Constitution gives people basic rights and limits the power of government. People vote for government officials who represent their interests.

2. • They vote for programs and laws that will help your neighborhood.
   • They work to improve the city, state, or country as a whole.
   • They respond to your telephone calls and letters.

Inside Information (p. 62)

I promise I will be loyal to the flag of the United States and to the country it represents. Our ancestors came from different countries. We live in different towns and states. But we are part of one nation—a nation that offers freedom and fairness to all.

13 Fall From Grace, Part 2

Remember the Story (pp. 66 and 67)

1 Amanda Hathaway to Carla Castillo
2. Roberto Sanchez to Carla Castillo
3. Mayor Reilly to Amanda Hathaway
4. Amanda Hathaway to Mayor Reilly
5. Ernesto to crowd of people
6. Roberto Sanchez to Amanda Hathaway

a. 5   b. 4   c. 1   d. 3   e. 2

1. demonstrators
2. chairing
3. petition
4. recall
5. supporters
6. registered
7. resign

Answers may vary. Here are some possible answers.

1. I don't know. They haven't done anything yet.

2. I was afraid. I thought I would lose my apartment.

3. She doesn't represent my interests.   OR
   I feel angry because she didn't tell the truth.

4. I am going to work for another candidate in the next election.   OR
   I am going to file a lawsuit to make her fix up the building.

Remember Turning Points (pp. 68 and 69)

1. T   2. F   3. T   4. F   5. T

Representative A: 1,   2,   6
Representative B: 1,   2,   5,   6

Answers may vary. Here are some possible answers.

1. • convince the elected official to resign from office

2. • contact the member of Congress and express concerns
   • circulate a recall petition
   • vote for another candidate in the next election

3. • investigate the member of Congress
   • impeach the member of Congress
   • vote to remove the congressperson from office

4. • investigate the member of Congress
   • write a news story or broadcast reports about the misuse of power

Making Connections (p. 69)

Councilwoman Amanda Hathaway

One City Council member suggests that she resign. Holcomb suggests that she take some time off and go on vacation. Mayor Reilly visits her at home and tells her that he thinks she should step down.

The tenants meet and decide to circulate petitions requesting a special recall election. If they can't get enough signatures, they may have to wait until the next election and then vote Hathaway out of office.

Find Out More: Key Ideas (p. 72)

1. **a.** Sometimes citizens also vote on issues, such as building schools or increasing local taxes.
2. **c.** Although many of the responsibilities of people in the United States are not required by law, they are essential for the common good—for the well-being of neighborhoods, towns, states, and the country.
3. **a.** But two important rights they don't have are the right to vote and the right to hold public office.
4. **b.** But in a democracy, citizens can freely ask questions and take part in the political community.

Answers may vary. Here are some possible answers.

1. voting, holding public office, working for the campaign of a candidate they support, and working for a cause they support.
2. pay taxes, defend the nation, appear as witnesses in court, and attend school.

Answers may vary. Here are some possible answers.

1. People can work for candidates and issues they support. They can vote in elections. They can volunteer to help with projects for the community. They can volunteer at a local school, help with a neighborhood clean-up campaign, or work with a Neighborhood Watch program.
2. Answers depend on your personal contributions to your neighborhood, to local education and civic programs, and to your employer.

14 Skin Deep

Remember the Story (pp. 78 and 79)

🔔
1. Police officer to Grace Ardmore
2. Derek Powell to Walter Prescott
3. Sam Hasharian to Carla Castillo
4. Mayor Reilly to Derek Powell and Jess Holcomb
5. Sam Hasharian to Walter Prescott
6. Nate Thompson to City Council

🔔🔔
a. 3   b. 1   c. 2   d. 5   e. 4

1. constituents
2. renovation
3. class-action lawsuit
4. disturbing the peace
5. relocate
6. health and safety violations

🔔🔔🔔
Answers may vary. Here are some possible answers.

1. I have to make money to support our family.

2. The law protects free enterprise. I have a legal business.   OR
   I pay taxes to support the city just like other business owners.   OR
   I can build a wall so my clients won't bother the other businesses.

3. It costs a lot of money to move.

4. We came here for a better life. I hope we succeed.

Remember Turning Points (pp. 80 and 81)

🔔
1. F   2. T   3. T   4. T   5. F

🔔🔔
Economic Reasons

2. crop failure
3. famine
4. loss of jobs

Other Reasons

1. political persecution
5. religious persecution
6. revolution
7. war

🔔🔔🔔
Answers may vary. Here are some possible answers.

1. abundance of land
   farmed the land

2. new mines and mills
   worked in the mines and mills

3. need for goods and services
   started businesses to meet needs

4. need for education
   started schools and taught

Making Connections (p. 81)

The immigrant, Sam Hasharian, runs a tattoo parlor because he can't support his family as an artist. (2 points)

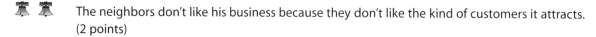

The neighbors don't like his business because they don't like the kind of customers it attracts. (2 points)

- The owner of the neighboring business, Grace Ardmore, tells Hasharian, the tattoo shop owner, that his business doesn't belong in the neighborhood. (1 point)
- The councilman from the district, Prescott, tells Powell he'd like the tattoo shop closed down, possibly because of health code violations. (1 point) OR
  Prescott visits the tattoo shop and suggests the business would grow faster if it were located somewhere more in keeping with Hasharian's line of work. (1 point)
- The Department of Health and Safety collects equipment and papers from the tattoo parlor and shuts it down temporarily until the investigation is complete. (1 point)
- The neighbors demonstrate in the street outside the tattoo parlor. They carry signs to protest ("Shut it down!") and suggest the parlor is a threat to health ("No AIDS here!"). (1 point)

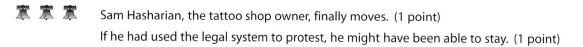

Sam Hasharian, the tattoo shop owner, finally moves. (1 point)

If he had used the legal system to protest, he might have been able to stay. (1 point)

Find Out More: Key Ideas (p. 84)

1. **b.** the Framers of the Constitution—the people who wrote the Constitution—wanted to be sure that the economy of the new nation could grow and be strong.
2. **a.** The states did not have the right to coin money or enter into treaties with foreign nations.
3. **a.** Someone who invents a new product or process has the right to protect that idea with a copyright or patent.
4. **c.** People have the right to join labor unions and professional associations.

Answers may vary. Here are some possible answers.

1. collect taxes, borrow money, regulate business, coin money, and regulate the value of money.
2. (any two of the following) establish and operate a business; buy, own, and sell property; choose the kind of work they do; change jobs; join a union or professional association; protect an invention with a copyright or patent.

🔔 🔔 🔔 Answers may vary. Here are some possible answers.

1. Congress coins all the money so all states can use the same kind of money. All the money has the same value. This makes it easy for businesses to operate in more than one state. It helps to promote business and strengthen the economy.

2. • People help the economy by creating goods and services that can be bought and sold. OR
   • People help the economy by supporting themselves and their families. OR
   • People help the economy by paying income, sales, and business taxes.

Inside Information (p. 86)

Answers may vary. Here are some possible answers.

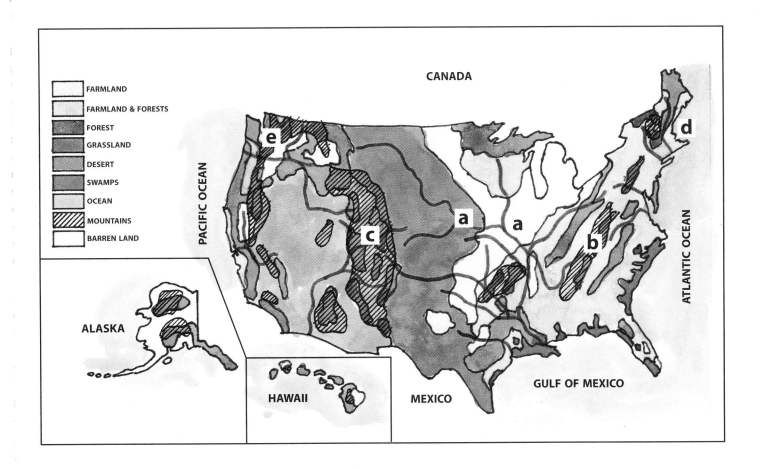

15 Hidden Agenda

Remember the Workers' Story (pp. 90 and 91)

1. Worker to Carla Castillo
2. Carla Castillo to TV audience
3. Jess Holcomb to Mayor Reilly and Derek Powell
4. Mr. Lee to Jess Holcomb
5. Supervisor to Older worker

a. 3   b. 2   c. 4   d. 1   e. 5

1. workplace abuse
2. overtime
3. competitor
4. contract
5. labor law
6. references

Answers may vary. Here are some possible answers.

1. I own a cleaning company.
2. I charge less than other companies.
3. I treat my employees very well.
4. Only one person complained at first.   OR
   They were not good workers.

Remember Katherine's Story (pp. 92 and 93)

1. Tom Hendricks to Katherine Morrison
2. Katherine Morrison to Tom Hendricks
3. John Sweeney to TV audience
4. Katherine Morrison to Tom Hendricks
5. Carla Castillo to Steve Richards

a. 2   b. 4   c. 3   d. 5   e. 1

1. violated
2. ethical
3. civil rights
4. alleges
5. discrimination
6. fires

Answers may vary. Here are some possible answers.

1. I was a TV news anchor.
2. They think I'm too old for the job.
3. My attorneys are filing a lawsuit against the television station.
4. It could hurt my chances. I may be considered a troublemaker.

Remember Turning Points (pp. 94 and 95)

1. b   2. c   3. b   4. a   5. c   6. a   7. c

1. discrimination
2. civil rights
3. unfair labor practices
4. protests
5. change
6. Goal: equal opportunities for all

Answers may vary. Here are some possible answers.

1. two people receive the same pay for the same job
2. the right to vote
3. companies have safe working environments
4. students demonstrate against an increase in tuition
5. law passed to prevent child labor

Making Connections (p. 95)

Unfair Labor Practices

 the cleaning company workers

no pay for overtime, forced to work when sick, no time to rest. These practices violate worker rights established by law.

The workers talked to Carla Castillo and the city attorney. They could have refused to work for Mr. Lee or tried to start their own cleaning service.

Discrimination

Katherine Morrison

She was fired because of her age. It is illegal to discriminate on the basis of age.

Katherine filed a lawsuit against the TV station. She could have tried to get an anchor position with another station.

Find Out More: Key Ideas (p. 98)

1. **b.** It allows for change through amendments that are agreed to by most of the states, through court rulings, and through the legislative process.
2. **b.** By law, she had to attend a school for black children twenty-one blocks away.
3. **c.** Because Ida Phillips had two preschool children, she was not hired.
4. **a.** Equal Pay Act—Fair Labor Standards Act, 1963. Prohibits discrimination in pay on the basis of sex.

Answers may vary. Here are some possible answers.

1. separate schools are not equal.   OR   separate schools harm both black and white children.
2. court decisions and public pressure.

1. As a result of the Linda Brown case, black and white children attend the same schools. As a result of the Ida Phillips case, companies cannot discriminate against women with children.
2. Answers come from personal experience.

Inside Information (p. 100)

Holiday and Date	Why this day is celebrated	Tradition
MARTIN LUTHER KING DAY (3rd Monday in January)	To honor the contributions of civil rights leader Dr. Martin Luther King, Jr.	Speeches and parades.
PRESIDENT'S DAY (3rd Monday in February)	To honor the contributions of Presidents George Washington and Abraham Lincoln.	Children study the presidents in school. Often adults get a day off work.
MEMORIAL DAY (4th Monday in May)	Originally to honor soldiers and sailors who died in the Civil War; now to honor all who have died fighting in wars.	Speeches and parades; placing of flowers on soldiers' graves. Many people have holidays from work and celebrate the start of summer with picnics.
LABOR DAY (1st Monday in September)	To honor working men and women.	People often get a day off work. Often celebrated with picnics and outings because it is considered the end of the summer season.
VETERANS DAY November 11	Originally to celebrate the anniversary of the end of World War I. Now to honor all men and women who have served in the armed forces.	Speeches and parades; holiday from work for some people.

Score Sheet for Answers for Exercises

After you check your answers, use the score sheet to record the number correct. Your teacher or tutor may want to see your scores.

Unit 8, Rules of the Game

	🔔	🔔🔔	🔔🔔🔔
Remember Anwar Khalil's Story	___ out of 5	___ out of 11	___ out of 4
Remember the Police Officers' Story	___ out of 5	___ out of 12	___ out of 4
Remember Turning Points	___ out of 5	___ out of 8	___ out of 6
Making Connections	___ out of 4	___ out of 4	___ out of 2
Find Out More: Key Ideas	___ out of 8	___ out of 2	___ out of 2

Unit 9, Sticks and Stones, Part 1

	🔔	🔔🔔	🔔🔔🔔
Remember the Story	___ out of 6	___ out of 10	___ out of 4
Remember Turning Points	___ out of 5	___ out of 6	___ out of 3
Making Connections	___ out of 3	___ out of 3	___ out of 4
Find Out More: Key Ideas	___ out of 8	___ out of 4	___ out of 4

Unit 10, Sticks and Stones, Part 2

	🔔	🔔🔔	🔔🔔🔔
Remember the Story	___ out of 5	___ out of 12	___ out of 4
Remember Turning Points	___ out of 5	___ out of 9	___ out of 4
Making Connections	___ out of 2	___ out of 4	___ out of 2
Find Out More: Key Ideas	___ out of 8	___ out of 2	___ out of 2

Unit 11, A House Divided

	🔔	🔔🔔	🔔🔔🔔
Remember the Story	___ out of 6	___ out of 12	___ out of 4
Remember Turning Points	___ out of 5	___ out of 5	___ out of 6
Making Connections	___ out of 4	___ out of 2	___ out of 3
Find Out More: Key Ideas	___ out of 8	___ out of 4	___ out of 3

Unit 12, Fall from Grace, Part 1

	🔔	🔔🔔	🔔🔔🔔
Remember the Story	___ out of 6	___ out of 13	___ out of 4
Remember Turning Points	___ out of 5	___ out of 4	___ out of 8
Making Connections	___ out of 1	___ out of 3	___ out of 1
Find Out More: Key Ideas	___ out of 8	___ out of 2	___ out of 2

Unit 13, Fall from Grace, Part 2

	🔔	🔔🔔	🔔🔔🔔
Remember the Story	___ out of 6	___ out of 12	___ out of 4
Remember Turning Points	___ out of 5	___ out of 7	___ out of 4
Making Connections	___ out of 1	___ out of 2	___ out of 2
Find Out More: Key Ideas	___ out of 8	___ out of 6	___ out of 2

Unit 14, Skin Deep

	🔔	🔔🔔	🔔🔔🔔
Remember the Story	___ out of 6	___ out of 6	___ out of 4
Remember Turning Points	___ out of 5	___ out of 7	___ out of 8
Making Connections	___ out of 2	___ out of 6	___ out of 2
Find Out More: Key Ideas	___ out of 8	___ out of 3	___ out of 2

Unit 15, Hidden Agenda

	🔔	🔔🔔	🔔🔔🔔
Remember the Workers' Story	___ out of 5	___ out of 11	___ out of 4
Remember Katherine's Story	___ out of 5	___ out of 11	___ out of 4
Remember Turning Points	___ out of 7	___ out of 6	___ out of 5
Making Connections:			
• Unfair Labor Practices	___ out of 1	___ out of 2	___ out of 2
• Discrimination	___ out of 1	___ out of 2	___ out of 2
Find Out More: Key Ideas	___ out of 8	___ out of 2	___ out of 2

8 Check Your Progress on *Rules of the Game*

 Check Your Memory

Answer the questions.

1. What does *due process of law* mean?

2. How are the Fifth and Fourteenth Amendments different?

3. What is *substantive due process*?

4. What is *procedural due process*?

5. How does due process protect people accused of breaking a law?

6. How have due process clauses affected Supreme Court rulings?

To check your answers, look on pages 158 and 159. Record your score here.

If your score is 4 or more points, go to 🔔🔔.

🔔🔔 Make It Real

Read the three situations and then answer these questions for each of them.

   a. Is the city following due process?

   b. Explain the reasons for your answer.

1. The city has a telephone hotline. People call the hotline to report the names of suspected drug dealers. The police immediately arrest anyone reported to the hotline.

2. The city government employs only city residents. All city employees live in the city. New employees must move into the city before they start work.

3. The city schools have a rule against girls wearing scarves or anything else on their heads to class. Some girls wear scarves or hats to cover their heads in school because of their religious beliefs.

To check your answers, look on page 159. Record your score here.

If your score is 4 or more points, go to 🔔🔔🔔.

You Be the Judge

Read the situation. Then answer the questions.

George stabbed another man in a fight. George asked Janet to testify at his trial. He asked her to say that he was with her when the stabbing occurred, which is not true. George is Janet's good friend, and she wants to help him.

1. What should Janet do? Circle the letter of the better solution.

    a. Testify that George was with her when the stabbing occurred.

    b. Tell George that she cannot testify at his trial.

2. Give reasons for your choice. _____

_____

_____

_____

3. Write one more solution. _____

_____

_____

_____

To check your answers, look on page 159. Record your score here. ☐

Turn to page 174 and record your scores for 🔔, 🔔🔔, *and* 🔔🔔🔔.

Rate Yourself

Rate yourself. Use Y *(Yes)*, S *(Some)*, or N *(No)*.

_____ 1. I understand this unit in general.

_____ 2. I know what *due process of law* means.

_____ 3. I understand the difference between substantive due process and procedural due process.

_____ 4. I understand that protecting individual rights may conflict with protecting the rights of society.

_____ 5. I can use what I have learned.

9 Check Your Progress on *Sticks and Stones, Part 1*

🔔 **Check Your Memory**

Answer the questions.

1. What is due process?

2. Give one reason why due process is important.

3. What is the focus of the Fourth through the Eighth Amendments?

4. What does "innocent until proven guilty" mean?

5. Tell one way that due process limits how law enforcement officials can investigate a crime.

6. Name one way the Sixth Amendment protects people accused of a crime.

To check your answers, look on page 160. Record your score here.

If your score is 4 or more points, go to 🔔 🔔.

🔔 🔔 **Make It Real**

Read the situation and answer the questions.

The police believe that Mr. Jones stole Mr. Saroyan's car.

1. What are Mr. Jones' due process rights?

2. What should the police do to protect Mr. Jones' rights?

3. What should the courts do to protect Mr. Jones' rights?

4. What are Mr. Saroyan's rights?

5. What should Mr. Saroyan expect from the police?

6. What should Mr. Saroyan expect from the courts?

To check your answers, look on page 161. Record your score here.

If your score is 4 or more points, go to 🔔 🔔 🔔.

You Be the Judge

Read the situation. Then answer the questions.

Mrs. Kan accuses Mrs. Smith of dumping garbage in Mrs. Kan's yard. Mrs. Smith denies it. They both belong to a block association—a group of neighbors that works to improve the neighborhood. Mrs. Kan and Mrs. Smith ask the block association for help in solving their problem. The block association wants to follow the due process ideas of the Constitution.

1. What should they do first? Circle the better solution.

   a. The block association should tell Mrs. Smith to stop dumping garbage in Mrs. Kan's yard.

   b. The block association should ask Mrs. Kan to provide evidence that Mrs. Smith dumped the garbage.

2. Give reasons for your choice. _____

   _____

   _____

   _____

3. Write one more solution. _____

   _____

   _____

   _____

To check your answers, look on page 161. Record your score here.

Turn to page 174 and record your scores for 🔔, 🔔🔔, and 🔔🔔🔔.

Rate Yourself

Rate yourself. Use Y *(Yes)*, S *(Some)*, or N *(No)*.

_____ 1. I understand this unit in general.

_____ 2. I know the purpose of the criminal justice system.

_____ 3. I understand the constitutional rights of a person suspected or accused of committing a crime.

_____ 4. I understand the importance of due process procedures in a constitutional democracy.

_____ 5. I can use what I have learned.

10 Check Your Progress on
Sticks and Stones, Part 2

Check Your Memory

Answer the questions.

1. What is the purpose of a trial?

2. When can a judge declare evidence inadmissible?

3. What are the two sides in most U.S. legal cases?

4. Why do attorneys question potential jurors?

5. What is the role of the jury?

6. Name four steps between an arrest and sentencing.

To check your answers, look on page 162. Record your score here.

If your score is 4 or more points, go to 🔔🔔.

Make It Real

Read the situations and answer the questions.

1. Several years ago, Eva Houston was assaulted. Eva identified the man that she believed committed the crime. He was charged but not convicted. Now Eva's husband, Glen, has been called for jury duty. The defendant in the case is accused of assault.

   a. Which side—the defense or the prosecution—may not want Glen on the jury? Why?

   b. Why would the other side want him on the jury?

2. John Robinson is a delivery person. He is being tried for burglary. The day before the burglary, Robinson made a delivery to the house that was burglarized. A witness testified that he saw Robinson at the house about the time of the burglary. Detectives testified that they found fingerprints matching Robinson's on the front door knocker. A friend of Robinson's testified that they were together at the time of the burglary. But during cross-examination, the prosecuting attorney mentioned this friend's criminal record.

   a. Should the jury convict Robinson or acquit him?

   b. Give two reasons.

   c. What principle of the criminal justice system guides this decision?

To check your answers, look on page 163. Record your score here.

If your score is 4 or more points, go to 🔔🔔🔔.

You Be the Judge

Read the situation. Then answer the questions.

Serving on a jury is an important civic responsibility. When citizens are called for jury duty, they are required to report. Kate Murphy has just received an order to appear for jury duty. She already served on a jury three years ago, and many of her friends have never served. It is not a good time for her to be away from work.

1. What should Kate do? Choose the better answer.

    a. Ignore the order and not appear.

    b. Request a postponement.

2. Give reasons for your choice. _____

    _____

    _____

3. Write one more solution. _____

    _____

    _____

To check your answers, look on page 163. Record your score here.

Turn to page 174 and record your scores for 🔔, 🔔🔔, and 🔔🔔🔔.

Rate Yourself

Rate yourself. Use Y *(Yes)*, S *(Some)*, or N *(No)*.

_____ 1. I understand this unit in general.

_____ 2. I understand the purpose of trials in U.S. courts of law.

_____ 3. I understand the arrest and pre-trial process.

_____ 4. I understand the roles of the defense, prosecution, judge, and jury in a trial.

_____ 5. I can use what I have learned.

11 Check Your Progress on *A House Divided*

🔔 **Check Your Memory**

Answer the questions.

1. Name one group that has the right to vote now, but didn't have that right in the early years of the United States.

2. What did the Fifteenth Amendment to the Constitution do?

3. What did the Nineteenth Amendment to the Constitution do?

4. How did the Vietnam War influence voting rights?

5. What is a primary election?

6. What is a general election?

To check your answers, look on page 164. Record your score here. ☐

If your score is 4 or more points, go to 🔔🔔.

🔔🔔 **Make It Real**

Who can vote? Check the appropriate column. If you check *No* or *Not sure*, write the reason.

Who	Able to Vote?			Reason
	Yes	No	Not sure	
1. John, an 18-year-old high school senior who is a citizen	☐	☐	☐	
2. Jamal, a legal resident alien who is in the military	☐	☐	☐	
3. Susan, a middle-aged mother of two who is a citizen but cannot read	☐	☐	☐	
4. Alfredo, an 85-year-old who uses a wheelchair and has never missed voting in an election	☐	☐	☐	
5. Fred, a citizen who is in prison for a felony	☐	☐	☐	
6. Beth, who registered for the last election but didn't vote	☐	☐	☐	

To check your answers, look on page 165. Record your score here. ☐

If your score is 4 or more points, go to 🔔🔔🔔.

You Be the Judge

Read the situation. Then answer the questions.

Voting allows people to influence their government. Jim Harvey is a citizen, but he doesn't vote very often. He travels a lot for his job and is often out of town on election day. He will be out of town for the next general election. The race between the two candidates for mayor is very close.

1. What should Jim do to influence the election results? Choose the better solution.

    a. request an absentee ballot and submit it before election day

    b. be sure his wife votes as he would

2. Give reasons for your choice. _____

    _____

    _____

    _____

3. Write one more solution. _____

    _____

    _____

    _____

To check your answers, look on page 165. Record your score here. ☐

Turn to page 174 and record your scores for 🔔, 🔔🔔, *and* 🔔🔔🔔.

Rate Yourself

Rate yourself. Use Y *(Yes)*, S *(Some)*, or N *(No)*.

_____ 1. I understand this unit in general.

_____ 2. I know how voting rights in the United States have expanded.

_____ 3. I know the requirements and procedures for voting in the United States.

_____ 4. I understand voter rights and responsibilities.

_____ 5. I can use what I have learned.

12 Check Your Progress on *Fall from Grace, Part 1*

🔔 Check Your Memory

Answer the questions.

1. What is a democracy?

2. What is one example of representative government?

3. What limits the power of government?

4. What is the purpose of government in the United States?

5. According to John Locke, what are the three basic rights of people?

6. What is one example of how history has influenced the political system in the United States?

To check your answers, look on page 166. Record your score here.

If your score is 4 or more points, go to 🔔🔔.

🔔🔔 Make It Real

Answer the questions.

1. In this unit, you learned that one of the influences on the U.S. government was the direct democracy of ancient Athens. In the United States, where is direct democracy most likely to be used? Why? What is used at other levels of government instead of direct democracy? Why?

2. The writers of the U.S. Constitution included two ideas from English history: government is limited to protecting basic rights of people, and government's authority depends on the consent of the governed. Kevin James represents the Fourth District on the City Council. It is a district with high unemployment and lots of crime. A month ago the city reduced its police force. Kevin's district has two fewer police officers on each shift. Now there is even more crime. The people in Kevin's district are very angry. What is government's responsibility to the people? What is Kevin's responsibility to the people? How can the people influence Kevin?

To check your answers, look on page 167. Record your score here.

If your score is 4 or more points, go to 🔔🔔🔔.

🔔 🔔 🔔 You Be the Judge

Read the situation. Then answer the questions.

The Kaminskys rent an apartment in a large building. They haven't had any water for several days, and they almost never have hot water. They haven't had garbage service for more than a month.

Here are some things that they can do:

 a. move

 b. do not pay rent to landlord, but deposit the rent in a separate account until the problem is fixed

 c. join other tenants in a rent strike, following the process in item b above

 d. report violations to their landlord in writing

 e. talk to a newspaper reporter, radio announcer, or television reporter

 f. report violations to the appropriate city department

 g. report violations to their representative on the City Council

Do these three things with the list above:

1. Check things that may help other tenants.

2. List in order the things you would do for the common good to resolve the problem for all the tenants.

   Tell why you chose that order.

3. a. When would the Kaminskys withhold rent?

   b. When would they move?

To check your answers, look on page 167. Record your score here.

Turn to page 174 and record your scores for 🔔, 🔔🔔, and 🔔🔔🔔.

Rate Yourself

Rate yourself. Use Y *(Yes)*, S *(Some)*, or N *(No)*.

_____ 1. I understand this unit in general.

_____ 2. I know how history influenced the kind of government the United States has.

_____ 3. I understand the concept of representative government.

_____ 4. I understand the concepts of limited government and consent of the governed.

_____ 5. I can use what I have learned.

Check Your Progress

13 Check Your Progress on
Fall from Grace, Part 2

🔔 Check Your Memory

Answer the questions.

1. What can people do if elected representatives misuse their power?

2. How can public officials control other public officials who misuse their position or power?

3. What can Congress do if a federal government official accused of violating the law refuses to resign?

4. What is one way people in the United States can participate in the political process?

5. What is one responsibility that both citizens and lawful permanent residents have?

6. What is one right that U.S. citizens have but lawful permanent residents do not have?

To check your answers, look on page 168. Record your score here. ☐

If your score is 4 or more points, go to 🔔 🔔 *.*

🔔 🔔 Make It Real

Answer the questions.

1. Over half of the registered voters in a state disagree with one of the state's U.S. senators on the issue of raising taxes. Give three ways these citizens can show their disagreement.

2. In the story, some tenants in Roberto's apartment building are not U.S. citizens. They could not vote to put Amanda Hathaway out of office. Give three reasons that they could circulate a petition and ask citizens to recall a city councilwoman.

To check your answers, look on page 169. Record your score here. ☐

If your score is 4 or more points, go to 🔔 🔔 🔔 *.*

mmon Ground

You Be the Judge

Read the situation. Then answer the questions.

Four members of the City Council and many citizens of Brownstown believe that their mayor should not be in office. Three months ago, Mayor Banes was arrested by police for possession of cocaine. He first denied the cocaine was his, but later he admitted to the public that he has a drug problem. He said that it has not affected his work as a city leader.

1. What can the community do about the problem? Circle the letter of the better solution.

    a. A group of citizens begin a city-wide campaign to collect 2000 signatures on a petition to force a recall election. Four City Council members approach the mayor at his home and ask him to resign.

    b. A group of citizens appear before the City Council. They support giving the mayor a second chance if he will enter a drug rehabilitation program for three months.

2. Give reasons for your choice. _____

    _____

    _____

    _____

3. Write one more solution. _____

    _____

    _____

    _____

To check your answers, look on page 169. Record your score here. ☐

Turn to page 174 and record your scores for 🔔, 🔔🔔, *and* 🔔🔔🔔.

Rate Yourself

Rate yourself. Use Y *(Yes)*, S *(Some)*, or N *(No)*.

_____ 1. I understand this unit in general.

_____ 2. I understand the responsibilities of elected officials to the people they represent.

_____ 3. I understand the role of citizens in the political process.

_____ 4. I know the process for removing officials from public office.

_____ 5. I can use what I have learned.

14 Check Your Progress on *Skin Deep*

Check Your Memory

Answer the questions.

1. Where are the only references in the U.S. Constitution to the economic rights of individuals?

2. Name two economic rights that people in the United States have.

3. Give an example of a violation of a person's economic rights.

4. Name two economic rights that the Constitution gives Congress.

5. Why have many people immigrated to the United States over the years?

6. How have immigrants contributed to the United States?

To check your answers, look on pages 170 and 171. Record your score here.

If your score is 4 or more points, go to 🔔🔔.

Make It Real

Answer the questions.

1. Name three ways that economic freedoms in the United States help to encourage immigration.

2. Which situation below is allowed under the Fifth and Fourteenth Amendments? Tell why.

   a. A man is arrested for manufacturing drugs in a home and delivering them to dealers in the city. After a court hearing, the government takes away his car and house.

   b. A councilwoman wants to buy a store. The store owner doesn't want to sell. Police take away the store and sell it to the councilwoman.

To check your answers, look on page 171. Record your score here.

If your score is 4 or more points, go to 🔔🔔🔔.

You Be the Judge

Read the situation. Then answer the questions.

The buildings on Fargot Street used to be empty. Then many Chinese immigrants opened shops there. Now the area is a busy commercial district. However, the shop owners don't have parking for their customers, and they are losing business.

1. What should they do? Circle the letter of the better solution.

   a. They should stop other people from opening businesses in the area.

   b. They should try to convince the city to build a public parking lot in the neighborhood.

2. Give reasons for your choice. _____

   _____

   _____

   _____

3. Write one more solution. _____

   _____

   _____

   _____

To check your answers, look on page 171. Record your score here. ☐

Turn to page 174 and record your scores for *.*

Rate Yourself

Rate yourself. Use Y *(Yes)*, S *(Some)*, or N *(No)*.

_____ 1. I understand this unit in general.

_____ 2. I understand why many immigrants came to the United States.

_____ 3. I know the economic rights the Constitution gives to Congress.

_____ 4. I know what economic rights people have in the United States.

_____ 5. I can use what I have learned.

15 Check Your Progress on *Hidden Agenda*

🔔 Check Your Memory

Give examples.

1. a value that people in the U.S. share

2. discrimination

3. an unfair labor practice

4. a protection against discrimination

5. a protection against unfair labor practices

6. how change happens in the U.S.

To check your answers, look on page 172. Record your score here. 🔲

If your score is 4 or more points, go to 🔔🔔.

🔔🔔 Make It Real

Read the situations and answer the questions.

1. Lisa, a young mother with two preschool-age children, applied for a job. The interviewer asked her if she had children. Lisa told him about her children. She didn't get the job.

   a. Should Lisa complain about sex discrimination? Why or why not?_____

   _____

   b. What court ruling applies? _____

   c. What else could Lisa do? _____

2. Mary Johnson was hired by her company a little more than ten years ago. A co-worker, Fred Temple, was hired a little less than ten years ago. Mary and Fred both have Master's degrees in business administration. Mary and Fred both got promotions about three years ago, and now both manage sections with eight people in them. Mary just discovered that Fred's salary is $8,000 a year higher than hers.

   a. Is the company breaking a law? _____

   b. If so, what legislation applies? _____

   c. Should Mary talk to her supervisor? Why or why not? _____

   _____

To check your answers, look on page 173. Record your score here. 🔲

If your score is 4 or more points, go to 🔔🔔🔔.

🔔🔔🔔 You Be the Judge

Read the situation. Then answer the questions.

Boris and Olga immigrated to the United States a few months ago. Their first language is Russian. Their son, Mikhail, is seven years old and in second grade. Mikhail attends an English-only school. None of the children in the school receive any instruction in their first languages. Boris and Olga think that Mikhail needs some instruction in Russian.

1. What should Boris and Olga do? Circle the better solution.

   a. Write a letter to the editor of the local paper and file a lawsuit against the school district.

   b. Talk to the school administrator and work with other parents who want first-language support for their children.

2. Give reasons for your choice. _____
   _____
   _____
   _____

3. Write one more solution. _____
   _____
   _____
   _____

To check your answers, look on page 173. Record your score here. ☐

Turn to page 174 and record your scores for 🔔, 🔔🔔, and 🔔🔔🔔.

Rate Yourself

Rate yourself. Use Y *(Yes)*, S *(Some)*, or N *(No)*.

_____ 1. I understand this unit in general.

_____ 2. I understand how the Constitution supports equal opportunities.

_____ 3. I understand how legislation protects people from unfair labor practices.

_____ 4. I know how peaceful protest can lead to change.

_____ 5. I can use what I have learned.

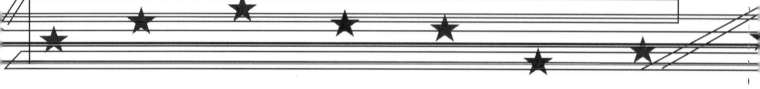

8 Answers for Check Your Progress on *Rules of the Game*

🔔 **Check Your Memory (p. 142)**

Each correct answer is worth 1 point. Check your answers. For any incorrect answer, review the information. If your score is 4 or more points, go to 🔔🔔.

	Answer	Review
1.	● The right to be treated fairly by the government ● Government cannot interfere with a person's right to life, liberty, or property without good and fair reasons.	Find Out More: Reading, What is due process of law?, p. 10 *Turning Points* video
2.	● The Fifth Amendment protects people from unfair and unreasonable treatment by the federal government. ● The Fourteenth Amendment extends the due process limitation to state governments.	Find Out More: Reading, What does the U.S. Constitution say about due process?, p. 10 *Turning Points* video
3.	● Substantive due process means that the content of laws that legislatures pass must be fair and reasonable. ● Congress and state legislatures cannot pass laws that interfere with what we believe, the kind of work we do, where we choose to live, or the friends we choose.	Find Out More: Reading, What is due process of law?, p. 10 *Turning Points* video Find Out More: Reading, What does the U.S. Constitution say about due process?, p. 10
4.	● Procedural due process means that the procedures, or methods, used to conduct hearings and to enforce the law must be fair and reasonable.	Find Out More: Reading, What is due process of law?, p. 10 *Turning Points* video
5.	● It says that they are presumed innocent unless proven guilty by a jury of their peers. ● There are strict rules about what evidence can be used and how it can be obtained.	Find Out More: Reading, What happens when the rights of the individual conflict with the rights of society?, p. 11

(continued)

	Answer	Review
6.	● The Supreme Court has used them to strengthen the idea of individual rights. ● The Supreme Court has used the Constitutional right to due process as the reason to overturn laws that unfairly threaten individual rights.	Find Out More: Reading, What does the U.S. Constitution say about due process?, p. 10

Make It Real (p. 142)

Each item is worth 2 points, 1 point for the answer to each question in the item. Answers may vary. Here are some possible answers.

1. No, the police cannot jail someone without evidence. First the police must conduct an investigation of the allegations.

2. Yes, the city wants employees who know about the city. Living in the city is a job requirement. People must move to the city if they want to work there.

3. No, laws and rules should not interfere with people's right to practice their religions.

You Be the Judge (p. 143)

Answers may vary. Here are some possible answers.

This question is worth 6 points, as follows:

    1 point for the better solution
    3 points for the reasons for your choices
    2 point for writing one more solution

1. **b.**

2. It is a crime to tell a lie in a court of law. The crime is perjury. A person who commits perjury may go to prison.

3. Answers will vary for other solutions. One possible solution is that she could help George find a good lawyer to represent him.

9 Answers for Check Your Progress on *Sticks and Stones, Part 1*

🔔 Check Your Memory (p. 144)

Each correct answer is worth 1 point. Check your answers. For any incorrect answer, review the information. If your score is 4 or more points, go to 🔔🔔.

	Answer	Review
1.	● the right to be treated fairly by government	Find Out More: Reading, How does the Constitution protect the rights of people accused of crimes?, p. 22
2.	● so that powerful governments cannot punish people for disagreeing with them	*Turning Points* video Find Out More: Reading, How does the Constitution protect the rights of people accused of crimes?, p. 22
3.	● protect the rights of people who are suspected, charged, or convicted of a crime	*Turning Points* video
4.	● The government must prove that the defendant is guilty beyond a reasonable doubt; defendants are not required to prove that they are innocent.	Find Out More: Reading, How does the Constitution protect the rights of people accused of crimes?, p. 22
5.	● allows the court to decide if police have enough evidence to hold a person ● requires a warrant to search people and seize property ● requires that bail and fines for people charged or convicted of crimes be fair and reasonable	Find Out More: Reading, Writ of Habeas Corpus, p. 22 Find Out More: Reading, Limits on Search and Seizure, p. 22 Find Out More: Reading, Bail, Fines, and Punishment, p. 23
6.	● the right to know the charges against you ● the right to a speedy and public trial ● the right to an impartial jury ● the right to be defended by legal counsel ● the right to force witnesses to appear in court ● the right to challenge what witnesses say	Find Out More: Reading, Right to a Fair Trial, p. 23

Make It Real (p. 144)

Each correct answer is 1 point. Answers may vary. Here are some possible answers.

1. Mr. Jones is "innocent until proven guilty." He has the right to a fair trial.

2. The police should get evidence to show that Mr. Jones is guilty before they arrest him. They need his permission or a warrant to search his house or take his property.

3. The courts should give Mr. Jones a speedy and public trial. Mr. Jones has the right to have an attorney represent him. The courts should allow Mr. Jones' attorney to call and cross-examine witnesses.

4. Mr. Saroyan has the right to protection from people who break the law.

5. He should expect the police to look for his stolen car and try to find the person who took it.

6. He should expect the courts to decide the innocence or guilt of the person charged with the crime and, if that person is convicted, decide what the punishment is.

You Be the Judge (p. 145)

This question is worth 6 points, as follows:

    1 point for the better solution
    3 points for the reasons
    2 point for writing one more solution

1. **b.**

2. They should assume that Mrs. Smith is innocent until they have enough evidence to prove that she is guilty. They might visit Mrs. Kan's yard to look for evidence of garbage dumping. They might look for proof that it is Mrs. Smith's garbage, such as mail addressed to her.

3. Answers will vary for other solutions. Here is one possible solution.

    The block association could form a "Keep Our Neighborhood Clean" committee and ask Mrs. Smith to serve on it.

10 Answers for Check Your Progress on *Sticks and Stones, Part 2*

🔔 Check Your Memory (p. 146)

Each correct answer is worth 1 point. Check your answers. For any incorrect answer, review the information. If your score is 4 or more points, go to 🔔🔔.

	Answer	Review
1.	● to determine the truth based on evidence; to prove innocence or guilt.	*Turning Points* video Find Out More: Reading, Conducting the trial, p. 35
2.	● when the defense attorney objects to how evidence was obtained and the judge finds it was obtained illegally	*Turning Points* video Video story
3.	● the prosecution ● the defense	*Turning Points* video Find Out More: Reading, Assigning a prosecutor and appointing a defense attorney, p. 34
4.	● to make sure they will be fair and impartial	*Turning Points* video Find Out More: Reading, Selecting a jury, p. 35
5.	● to listen to the evidence ● to discuss the case after all the evidence has been presented ● to decide on a verdict	Video story *Turning Points* video Find Out More: Reading, Reaching a verdict, p. 35
6.	● arresting a suspect ● booking the suspect ● deciding which court ● assigning a prosecutor ● holding the preliminary hearing ● appointing a defense attorney ● setting bail ● entering a plea ● examining the evidence ● offering to plea bargain ● selecting a jury ● conducting the trial ● reaching a verdict ● determining the sentence	Find Out More: Reading, pp. 34 and 35

Make It Real (p. 146)

Answers may vary. Here are some possible answers.

1. **a.** the defense, because Glen may still be angry about his wife's experience and have difficulty being impartial (1 point)

    b. the prosecution, because he may be partial toward the victim, and not toward the defendant (1 point)

2. **a.** acquit (1 point)

    b. The fingerprints on the door knocker could be there from Robinson's delivery rather than from a burglary. Also, it is wrong to assume that Robinson's friend is perjuring himself just because he has a criminal record. (2 points)

    c. reasonable doubt (1 point)

You Be the Judge (p. 147)

This question is worth 6 points, as follows:

  1 point for the better solution
  3 points for the reason(s)
  2 points for writing one more solution

1. **b.**

2. U.S. citizens are required to report for jury duty. They can request a delay, but only the court can excuse them. Ignoring the summons could create problems.

3. Answers will vary for other solutions. One possible solution is that Kate could make arrangements with her employer to do work nights and evenings and during breaks in the trial.

11 Answers for Check Your Progress on *A House Divided*

🔔 Check Your Memory (p. 148)

Each correct answer is worth 1 point. Check your answers. For any incorrect answer, review the information. If your score is 4 or more points, go to 🔔🔔.

	Answer	Review
1.	• black males • women • adults between 18 and 21	*Turning Points* video
2.	• It gave full citizenship to blacks and guaranteed males the right to vote, regardless of race, color, or whether they had been slaves.	*Turning Points* video
3.	• It gave women the right to vote.	*Turning Points* video
4.	• People felt that if men could be drafted at 18 to fight for their country, they should be able to vote for or against members of Congress who approve the country's involvement in the war.	*Turning Points* video
5.	• Members of a political party choose that party's candidates for office.	Find Out More: Reading, What is the difference between a primary election and a general election?, p. 46
6.	• Voters make final decisions about candidates and issues.	Find Out More: Reading, What is the difference between a primary election and a general election?, p. 46

Make It Real (p. 148)

This question is worth 6 points, 1 point for each correct check AND reason

1. Yes. Eighteen-year-olds can vote if registered.

2. No. Jamal is not a citizen.

3. Yes. Literacy is not a requirement to vote.

4. Yes. Alfredo registered and can vote by absentee ballot.

5. No. People who have been convicted of a felony and are in prison or on parole are not allowed to vote.

6. Not sure. It depends on the state. She may have to reregister in order to vote.

You Be the Judge (p. 149)

This question is worth 6 points, as follows:

   1 point for the better solution
   3 points for the reason(s)
   2 points for writing one more solution

1. **a**

2. If Jim votes by absentee ballot, he won't have to miss work. His wife should be able to vote for the candidate she chooses. That candidate may not be the same one her husband chooses.

3. Answers will vary for other solutions. One possible solution is that he could reschedule his business trip.

12 Answers for Check Your Progress on *Fall from Grace, Part 1*

Check Your Memory (p. 150)

Each correct answer is worth 1 point. Check your answers. For any incorrect answer, review the information. If your score is 4 or more points, go to 🔔🔔.

	Answer	Review
1.	• government by the people and for the people • rule by people	*Turning Points* video Find Out More: Reading, The Democracy of Ancient Athens, p. 58
2.	• senators in ancient Rome • City Council members • state and national legislatures	*Turning Points* video Find Out More: Reading, The Representative Government of Rome, p. 58 Video story
3.	• the consent of the people • the U.S. Constitution	*Turning Points* video Find Out More: Reading, The English Tradition, p. 59
4.	• to protect basic rights of the people	*Turning Points* video Find Out More: Reading, The English Tradition, p. 59
5.	• the right to life, liberty, and property	*Turning Points* video Find Out More: Reading, The English Tradition, p. 59
6.	• the concept of democracy from ancient Athens • the concept of representative government from ancient Rome • the concept of basic rights from the English tradition • the concept of limited government from the English tradition	Find Out More: Reading, pp. 58 and 59

Make It Real (p. 150)

Each item is worth 3 points; 1 point for the answer to each question within the item. Answers may vary. Here are some possible answers.

1 Direct democracy is more likely to be used in small towns and villages where there are few people. In a direct democracy, people vote directly on all issues that affect their town. At the state and national levels of government in the United States, citizens elect representatives to serve their interests and govern the state or nation. This form of representative democracy is much more practical than trying to have the people themselves make all the decisions.

2. It is government's responsibility to protect the people's basic rights, which include property rights. It is Kevin's responsibility to represent the interests of the people in the Fourth District and the city as a whole. If the cutback in police protection has occurred only in this one district, people should certainly contact Kevin. If it is a city-wide cutback, they might still meet with him and other groups in the city to discuss other solutions. These might include Neighborhood Watch and other crime-prevention programs. Finally, the people can choose not to support Kevin in the next election if he is not serving their interests.

You Be the Judge (p. 151)

1. c. e. f. g. (1 point)

2. d. f. g. c. e. (1 point)

This order moves from people most responsible for the problem to people with least responsibility, as well as from the least public to the most public. (2 points)

3. If the Kaminskys feel the problem is theirs alone, withholding rent and depositing it in a separate account may be a way to get the landlord to fix the water problem. (1 point)

   If they feel that there will be no change in the situation whatever they do, they might choose to move. (1 point)

13 Answers for Check Your Progress on *Fall from Grace, Part 2*

🔔 Check Your Memory (p. 152)

Each correct answer is worth 1 point. Check your answers. For any incorrect answer, review the information. If your score is 4 or more points, go to 🔔🔔.

	Answer	Review
1.	• try to recall them by circulating petitions for a recall election • vote them out of office in the next election	Video story *Turning Points* video
2.	• talk them into resigning	Video story *Turning Points* video
3.	• investigate the misuse of power, impeach, and remove official from office if the charges are proved	*Turning Points* video
4.	• by voting • by running for office • by working on campaigns • by serving in appointed positions • by joining special interest groups	Find Out More: Reading, How do U.S. citizens exercise political power?, p. 70
5.	• to pay taxes • to defend the nation • to appear as a witness in court • to attend school	Find Out More: Reading, What are the rights and responsibilities of people who live in the United States?, p. 71
6.	• the right to vote • the right to hold public office • the right to serve on a jury	Find Out More: Reading, What are the rights and responsibilities of people who live in the United States?, p. 71

Make It Real (p. 152)

Each correct answer is worth 3 points. Answers may vary. Here are some possible answers.

1. a. calling or writing to the senator

    b. not reelecting the senator in the next election

    c. coming together in public protest

2. a. The poor condition of the apartment building violates basic human rights and is a danger to the general public.

    b. The tenants want to let voters know about the councilwoman's dishonesty.

    c. Councilwoman Hathaway is one of the owners of the apartment building, so she should be held partly responsible for its condition.

You Be the Judge (p. 153)

This question is worth 6 points, as follows:

    1 point for the better solution
    3 points for the reasons
    2 points for writing one more solution

1. **a** is the better solution.

2. Mayor Banes' drug addiction will get in the way of his ability to perform the duties of his office. Possession and use of cocaine is illegal. The mayor will be charged and tried for this offense.

3. Answers will vary for other solutions. One possible solution is to let the mayor remain in office until the end of his term and elect someone else in the next election.

14 Answers for Check Your Progress on *Skin Deep*

🔔 Check Your Memory (p. 154)

Each correct answer is worth 1 point. Check your answers. For any incorrect answer, review the information. If your score is 4 or more points, go to 🔔🔔.

	Answer	Review
1.	• the Fifth Amendment • the Fourteenth Amendment	Find Out More: Reading, What economic rights do people have in the United States?, p. 82
2.	the right to: • seek copyright and patent protection • join labor unions and professional associations • choose the kind of work they do and change jobs • buy, own, and sell property • establish and operate a business	Find Out More: Reading, What economic rights do people have in the United States?, p. 82
3.	• forcing a person to move his place of business • forbidding a person to join a union • not allowing a person to buy, own, or sell property • not allowing a person to choose or change jobs	Video story Find Out More: Reading, What economic rights do people have in the United States?, p. 82
4.	the power to: • collect taxes • borrow money • regulate business between states and with other nations • coin money and regulate its value	Find Out More: Reading, What economic powers does the Constitution give Congress?, p. 82

(continued)

	Answer	Review
5.	● because of economic difficulties in their own countries and opportunities in the United States	*Turning Points* video *Turning Points* video
6.	● farmed the land ● built railroads ● worked in mills ● started businesses ● invented new products and processes ● educated others	

Make It Real (p. 154)

Answers may vary. Here are some possible answers.

1. Many people come to the United States in search of better jobs or a better life. In the United States, people have the right to own businesses and personal property. U.S. laws also protect the rights of workers. These rights help the economy grow. When the economy grows, new opportunities are created for workers and business owners. Many immigrants benefit from these opportunities.

2. Situation **a** is allowed under the Fifth and Fourteenth Amendments. (1 point)
   The government can take away a person's property if the property was used for criminal purposes; it is allowed by law. Situation **b** is not allowed because no person can lose property without due process of law. (2 points)

You Be the Judge (p. 155)

Answers may vary. Here are some possible answers. This question is worth 6 points, as follows:

   1 point for the better solution
   3 points for the reasons
   2 points for writing one more solution.

1. **b.**

2. If the business owners can work together to solve the parking problem, they will all benefit. Other business owners have a right to establish their businesses even if it causes more traffic congestion.

3. Answers will vary for other solutions. One possible solution is that the business owners could work together and combine their money to build a parking lot for customers.

15 Answers for Check Your Progress on *Hidden Agenda*

🔔 **Check Your Memory (p. 156)**

Each correct answer is worth one point. Check your answers. For any incorrect answer, review the information. If your score is 4 or more points, go to 🔔🔔.

	Answer	Review
1.	• equal opportunities • civil rights • fair labor practices • the right to non-violent protest of unfair practices	Video story *Turning Points* video Find Out More: Reading, How have court rulings helped to increase equal opportunities?, p. 96
2.	• age discrimination • racial discrimination • discrimination on the basis of sex	Video story *Turning Points* video Find Out More: Reading, How have court rulings helped to increase equal opportunities?, p. 96
3.	• no pay for overtime • forced to work when sick • no time to rest • poor working conditioins	Video story *Turning Points* video
4.	• Fourteenth Amendment to the Constitution • legislation • court rulings	Video story
5.	• legislation	Find Out More: Reading, What contributions has legislation made?, p. 97
6.	• through protest • through court rulings • through legislation	Find Out More: Reading, How have court rulings helped to increase equal opportunities?, p. 96 Find Out More: Reading, What contributions has legislation made?, p. 97

Make It Real (p. 156)

Each item is worth 3 points, 1 for the answer to each question. Answers may vary. Here are some possible answers.

1. a. no, because she doesn't have enough information. *If* the intervewer asked men the same question, it is not discrimination based on sex.

   b. the Ida Phillips case against Martin Marietta Corporation

   c. get more information about the interview process and the company

2. a. probably it is

   b. Equal Pay Act of the Fair Labor Standards Act

   c. yes, if she and Fred do equal work and are equally qualified but do not receive equal pay

You Be the Judge (p. 157)

Answers may vary. Here are some possible answers. This question is worth 6 points, as follows:

   1 point for the better solution
   3 points for the reasons
   2 points for writing one more solution

1. **b.**

2. **b** is the approach. It encourages people with shared values to work together and is less likely to result in a conflict. Choice **a** would be expensive and would cause conflict. Steps like **a** should not be taken until all other approaches have been considered.

3. Answers will vary for other solutions. One possible solution is that Boris and Olga could join with other Russian families to explore ways for their children to speak Russian outside of school.

Score Sheet for Answers for Check Your Progress

	Check Your Memory (6 points)	Make It Real (6 points)	You Be the Judge (6 points)
Unit 8 Rules of the Game	_____	_____	_____
Unit 9 Sticks and Stones, Part 1	_____	_____	_____
Unit 10 Sticks and Stones, Part 2	_____	_____	_____
Unit 11 A House Divided	_____	_____	_____
Unit 12 Fall from Grace, Part 1	_____	_____	_____
Unit 13 Fall from Grace, Part 2	_____	_____	_____
Unit 14 Skin Deep	_____	_____	_____
Unit 15 Hidden Agenda	_____	_____	_____

acquit to clear a person of a charge by declaring him or her not guilty 4

administration executive branch of government 43

alibi proof that someone was not at the scene of a crime and, therefore, not guilty of the crime 5

allegation statement offered but not yet proved 55

allege to state without proof 92

Amendment change in or addition to the U.S. Constitution 10

appeal request for a higher court to review a lower court's decision 22

arrest to take into or keep in custody by authority of law 7

assault and battery violent attack intended to hurt someone 18

bail money or other security given for a person's release from jail while he or she awaits trial 23

ballot document used to record a vote. In U.S. elections, votes are recorded on a secret ballot 47

basic rights fundamental rights to life, liberty, and property 59

Bill of Rights the first ten amendments to the U.S. Constitution, which restrict the federal government's power to interfere with certain basic rights of the people 10

book to officially charge someone with a crime 34

campaign organized effort to achieve a result, particularly a candidate's election to public office 42

candidate person seeking public office 48

chairing act of presiding over a meeting 67

challenger person opposing an incumbent in an election 43

charge official statement accusing someone of a crime 7

circumstantial appearing believable but unable to be proven 5

citizen member of a country or state; one who owes allegiance to the government and is entitled to its protection and to political rights 46

civil rights fundamental rights belonging to every member of a society 92

class-action lawsuit problem that a group of people take to a court of law 79

common good what is best for the entire society 71

competitor company or person that tries to be more successful than others that offer the same products or services 90

comply obey a request, order, law, or standard 54

Congress legislature of the United States, consisting of the Senate and the House of Representatives 97

consent of the governed an agreement by the people to set up and live under a government 59

constituents people who live in an elected official's district or area 79

Constitution set of customs, traditions, rules, and laws that set forth the way a government is organized and operated 10

contract legal agreement between two or more people or companies that tells what each side must do for the other 91

convict to find someone guilty in a court of law 19

copyright exclusive legal right to print, publish, perform, film, or record material 83

counsel person who gives legal advice and represents people accused of crimes; attorney, lawyer 23

court ruling judicial decision 96

cross-examine to ask a witness questions about something the witness testified to under oath in a court of law 19

defense lawyers representing the person accused of a crime in a court of law 31

defense attorney lawyer representing the person accused of a crime in a court of law   34

democracy form of government in which political control is exercised by the people, either directly, or indirectly through their elected representatives   71

demonstrator person who protests or supports something in public   66

dictatorship government controlled by one person with unlimited power   71

direct democracy government in which laws are made by the people themselves   58

discrimination unfair treatment, especially because of race, religion, age, or sex   92

disturbing the peace annoying, interfering with, or disrupting the activities of others   78

document formal letter, contract, or record   55

due process of law idea that every person is entitled to fair treatment by government, and that laws and procedures must be fair   10

election process of selecting public officials   42

endanger to expose to danger, loss, or peril   11

equal protection under the law idea that no individual or group may receive special privileges nor be unjustly discriminated against by the law   96

ethical relating to principles of right and wrong   93

evidence something legally submitted to a court of law to determine the truth of a matter   5

felony major crime such as murder or robbery   46

fine money paid to an injured party in a civil lawsuit   23

fire to end a person's employment   93

Framers the fifty-five men who attended the Constitutional Convention in 1887 and were instrumental in writing the Constitution of the United States   82

general election election following a primary election in which voters make final decisions about candidates and issues   46

guilty judged to have committed a specified crime   22

harass to annoy or torment someone   19

health and safety violation failure to keep an area clean and safe   78

illegal search searching a person's home, car, or other property without obtaining permission or having a warrant signed by a judge   7

impartial not favoring one person or group   23

inadmissible not accepted; not allowed   31

innocent not guilty of a crime   22

jury group of people who listen to details of a court case and decide whether the accused is innocent or guilty   30

justice system by which people are judged in courts of law and criminals are punished   4

labor laws rules made by government to protect the rights of workers against unfair treatment and acts of abuse   91

lawful permanent resident person who is authorized to live permanently in the United States, but is not a citizen   71

lawsuit legal action that takes a problem or claim to a court of law; case brought before a court   23

leave of absence permission to be absent from duty, employment, or service   43

legislation laws passed by Congress or state legislatures under powers granted by the Constitution   96

legislative process method by which Congress and state law-making bodies enact laws   96

limited government government whose power is restricted by law and by the will of the people through free and periodic elections   59

Magna Carta contract signed in 1215 between King John of England and his nobles. The agreement required the king to obey the law, and it gave certain rights to the nobility   59

Miranda rights (Miranda warning) rights read to the accused by police during the arrest procedure and stating that the accused has a right to remain silent and have an attorney present during questioning   18, 34

negligent extremely careless; not responsible   55

offense crime   23

overtime extra hours of work beyond the standard day or week   91

patent official document that gives the right to make, use, or sell an invention   83

peer person who is one's equal in age, rank, ability, or other quality   11

penalty punishment for breaking a law   55

perjury crime of deliberately giving false, misleading, or incomplete testimony under oath   7

petition formal written request to an official person or organization   66

plea bargain to plead guilty in exchange for a less serious charge or a shorter sentence   35

political party organization that seeks to achieve political power by electing members to public office   46

polling place place where people vote   47

primary election election in which members of the party choose their party's candidates for office   46

probable cause logical reasons for believing that someone accused of a crime is guilty   34

procedural due process idea that the procedures or methods used to carry out governmental responsibilities, conduct hearings, and enforce the law must be fair and reasonable   10

prosecuting attorney lawyer representing the state in a case against a person charged with a crime   34

prosecution lawyers representing the state in a case against a person charged with a crime   31

public office elected position in government   70

public pressure influence used by people to achieve a goal   97

reasonable doubt the basis for innocence in the justice system in the United States; a lack of certainty about the guilt of the accused   22

recall procedure by which a public official may be removed from office by popular vote during his or her term   66

references recommendations from someone who used services of a company or person   90

registered officially able to vote   67

renovation improvement made by repairing or remodeling a building or neighborhood   78

representative democracy system of government in which power is held by the people and exercised indirectly through elected representatives   58

resign to give up an office or position   66

search warrant order by a judge that authorizes a police officer to search a specific place   31

sentence legal punishment set by a court for someone judged guilty of a crime   23

speedy and public trial guarantee that the accused must be brought to trial within a reasonable period of time, and that people in the community can attend the trial   23

standard basis against which other things are measured   54

substantive due process idea that the content or substance of laws passed by legislatures must not unfairly limit a person's right to life, liberty, or property   10

supporter person in favor of a particular person, group, or plan   66

suspect person believed to be responsible for a crime   34

system rules, traditions, and government that influence people's lives   42

testify to give information under oath in a court of law   6

third parties political parties representing minority views and causes. Often third-party causes and issues are later adopted by the major parties   46

treaties formal agreements between countries   82

trial (criminal) formal event in which a judge and/or jury hear testimony and examine evidence to decide the guilt or innocence of the accused   22

verdict official decision by a jury in a court of law about whether someone is guilty   4

victim someone affected by a crime   5

violate to act against the law   93

violation act of breaking a rule or law   54

warrant official paper that allows the police to do something   22

witness person called to give evidence before a court   30

workplace abuse unfair treatment of employees by someone in authority   91

Unit 8: Rules of the Game

Family with boxes moving in to new house. *SuperStock.*
Man with gun coming through open window. *SuperStock.*
Men reading in synagogue. *PeterTurnley/(c) Corbis.*
People lined up at Opportunity Job Center. *AP/Wide World Photos.*
Man in handcuffs being led to car by officer. *American Stock Photography.*

Unit 9: Sticks and Stones, Part I

Policeman beats rioter in Harlem. *UPI/Corbis-Bettmann.*
Oklahoma City police chaplain comforts woman. *AP/Wide World Photos.*
Hand being fingerprinted by police. *John Running/Stock, Boston/PNI.*

Unit 10: Sticks and Stones, Part 2

Courtroom scene. *Jane O'Neal*

Unit 11: A House Divided

Balloons at Republican Convention. *Philip Gould/Corbis*

Unit 12: Fall from Grace, Part 1

Public square in ancient Greece. *Corbis.*
Session of the Roman Senate. *Corbis-Bettmann.*
Rome, Italy, A scene at the Roman Senate. *Corbis-Bettmann.*
King John signing the Magna Carta. *The Bettmann Archive.*
Detail of public square in ancient Greece. *Corbis.*
Title page from "Two Treatises of Government, John Locke." *William Andrews Clark Memorial Library, University of California, Los Angeles.*
British philosopher John Locke (colored engraving by Freeman from a painting by Sir Godfrey Kneller). *Corbis-Bettmann.*
Facsimile of the Magna Carta. *Corbis-Bettmann.*
Children pledging allegiance to flag. *Stephanie Maze/Corbis.*
Members of the United States Women's Olympic Ice Hockey Team recite Pledge of Allegiance. *AP/Wide World Photos.*
Woman from Taiwan recites Pledge of Allegiance at a naturalization ceremony. *AP/Wide World Photos.*
Pledge of Allegiance at town meeting. *Nathan Benn/Corbis.*

Unit 13: Fall from Grace, Part 2

Ballot Box. *Joseph Sohm; ChromoSohm Inc./Corbis.*
Public official serving constituents. *Michael Elderman.*
Same public official meeting with an industrial leader. *Michael Elderman.*
Same public official in the chamber. *Source unknown.*

Unit 14: Skin Deep

Scrubwoman, New York City, 1920. *Courtesy George Eastman House.*
Man in doorway of grocery store. *Shades Of L. A. Archives, Los Angeles Public Library.*
Man and boy in barber shop, 1929. *Shades Of L. A. Archives, Los Angeles Public Library.*
Chinese railroad workers, Promontory, Utah. *Denver Public Library, Western Collection/Union Pacific Museum Collection.*

Unit 15: Hidden Agenda

Boys replacing bobbins. *Courtesy of the Library of Congress.*

Women suffragists picket in front of the White House. *Courtesy of the Library of Congress.*

Children at the Manzanar internment camp in California. *AP/Wide World Photos.*

United Farm Workers President Cesar Chavez addressing a meeting. *Archives of Labor and Urban Affairs, Wayne State University.*

Linda Brown Smith as 9-year-old, Brown et al. vs. Board of Education, 1954. *AP/Wide World Photos.*

Mrs. Ida Phillips, job discrimination suit. *AP/Wide World Photos.*

"The First Thanksgiving" by Jerome Brownscombe. *Corbis-Bettmann.*

"Fireworks in the County." *Corbis-Bettmann.*